Fodor's

25 Best

D0423797

BARCELONA

How to Use This Book

KEY TO SYMBOLS

➕ Map reference to the accompanying fold-out map

✉ Address

☎ Telephone number

🕐 Opening/closing times

🍽 Restaurant or café

🚃 Nearest rail station

Ⓜ Nearest subway (Metro) station

🚌 Nearest bus route

⛴ Nearest riverboat or ferry stop

♿ Facilities for visitors with disabilities

❓ Other practical information

▷ Further information

ℹ Tourist information

✋ Admission charges:
Expensive (over €9),
Moderate (€3–€9), and
Inexpensive (€2 or less)

★ Major Sight   ★ Minor Sight

👣 Walks   🚌 Drives

🛍 Shops

🎭 Entertainment and Nightlife

🍽 Restaurants

This guide is divided into four sections

• Essential Barcelona: An introduction to the city and tips on making the most of your stay.
• Barcelona by Area: We've broken the city into five areas, and recommended the best sights, shops, entertainment venues, nightlife and restaurants in each one. Suggested walks help you to explore on foot.
• Where to Stay: The best hotels, whether you're looking for luxury, budget or something in between.
• Need to Know: The info you need to make your trip run smoothly, including getting about by public transport, weather tips, emergency phone numbers and useful websites.

Navigation In the Barcelona by Area chapter, we've given each area its own colour, which is also used on the locator maps throughout the book and the map on the inside front cover.

Maps The fold-out map accompanying this book is a comprehensive street plan of Barcelona. The grid on this fold-out map is the same as the grid on the locator maps within the book. We've given grid references within the book for each sight and listing.

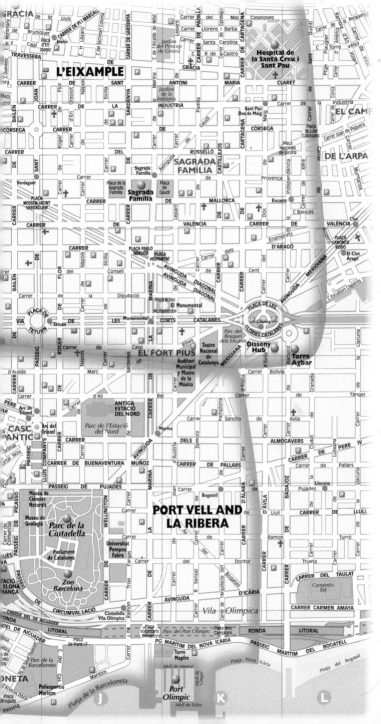

Contents

Introducing Barcelona

Self-confident, prosperous and buzzing Barcelona, capital of the autonomous Spanish region of Catalonia, is one of Europe's most compelling cities, pulling in millions of annual visitors who flock here to experience its style and diversity.

So, what's it got? The answer is something for everyone: stunning architecture, fine museums, excellent shopping, some inspirational food, and great cafés and nightlife. Not to mention the bonus of the city's seafront position, its medieval core, spacious boulevards and surrounding green hills.

The last decades have seen huge social, cultural and economic changes, with the physical reality of the city being changed by vast and ongoing building projects and Barcelona's role as Catalan capital becoming increasingly important. Economically, the local industry contributes a good percentage of Spain's overall output, coining in the profits to both the private and public sector. The powers-that-be spend the money relatively wisely, with the innovative 'Barcelona Model', where public and private spending are seamlessly mixed,

hailed by urban planners everywhere. But the flip side of this regeneration has been the dramatic rise in the cost of housing, with prices increasing by more than 60 per cent in the last decade, then plummeting again during the economic downturn. Young couples are moving out to the sprawling satellite settlements. This is putting pressure on small city businesses, with traditional shops being replaced by tourist-friendly outlets.

Since the 1960s the city has seen a huge influx of immigrants, both from other parts of Spain and from North Africa and South America. Assimilation has progressed relatively smoothly, though it's been an effort for a small city that has until recently struggled itself to keep its Catalan identity. Factors like these make Barcelona a stylish, 21st-century metropolis, with a unique edge that adds to its allure.

Facts + Figures

- Population: 1,615,908
- Area: City 99sq km (38sq miles)
- Highest point in Barcelona: Tibidabo (542m/1,777ft)
- The Port of Barcelona welcomed more than 2,408,000 passengers in 2012
- More than 7.5 million tourists visited the city in 2012

NO BULL

Bullfighting has been banned in Catalonia since 2012. It is not traditionally part of Catalan culture, and audiences had been dwindling for many years. One of its bullrings, Les Arenes, was converted into a swish shopping and entertainment complex designed by Richard Rogers, while the fate of the other, La Monumental, remains uncertain.

CLIMBING THE CASTLE

Seize the chance to catch the *castellers*, clubs of locals who build human castles up to 10 levels during the city's *La Merce* festival (23–27 Sep). Participants climb upon each other's shoulders to form 15m (50ft) constructions, traditionally topped by a child of 5 or 6, the *anxaneta*. The real heroes are the stalwarts taking the strain at the bottom level.

THE CITY NEVER SLEEPS

In Barcelona meals are taken later than in most other European cities. Bars don't really start buzzing until 11pm and clubs rarely see clients before midnight. Of course they sleep off the evening's revelries the next morning, right? Wrong! A 2009 study concluded the Spanish work on average 230 hours per year more than other Europeans, yet are lagging in terms of productivity.

A Short Stay in Barcelona

DAY 1

Morning Start your day in the **Barri Gòtic** (▷ 49), taking in the **Catedral** (▷ 42–43), the **Plaça de Sant Jaume** (▷ 51) and the **Plaça del Rei** (▷ 44–45), where, if your imagination's fired by the sense of history, you can learn more at the **Museu d'Història de Barcelona** (▷ 44). By 11.30, things are livening up on the **Ramblas** (▷ 46–47), so stroll up and down, pausing for a coffee, to soak up the atmosphere of Barcelona's most iconic thoroughfare. Take in the flower-sellers and street entertainers and then, if you've got the energy, walk along the waterfront beside the **Port Vell** (▷ 68–69) before heading up Via Laietana and turning right into the **Ribera** (▷ 73), one of Barcelona's oldest but coolest areas.

Lunch Enjoy a quintessentially Spanish lunch of freshly prepared tapas at **Taller de Tapas** (▷ 58) on Carrer de l'Argentería.

Afternoon Head down the street for the Plaça Santa Maria and spend a quiet moment in the beautiful Gothic church of **Santa Maria del Mar** (▷ 70–71) before heading up Carrer Montcada, one of the old city's loveliest streets, to visit the **Museu Picasso** (▷ 63), housed in a series of stunning late medieval merchants' houses.

Dinner Cross the Via Laietana and head through Carrer Jaume I and down Carrer Ferran for a drink at an outdoor table in the elegant **Plaça Reial** (▷ 51) before sampling a real Catalan dinner at **Can Culleretes** (▷ 57) just up the street, where classic local cooking has been served since 1786.

Evening Walk north through the old city, or take a taxi, to enjoy a performance in the stunning *modernista* surroundings of the **Palau de la Música Catalana** (▷ 64).

DAY 2

Morning Take the red-route Bus Turístic in the **Plaça de Catalunya** (▷ 50–51) and sit back for the half-hour or so ride to **Montjuïc** (▷ 30). Alight at the **Museu Nacional d'Art de Catalunya** (▷ 31), pausing on the terrace to take in the city views. Spend a couple of hours in the museum, perhaps concentrating on the superb Romanesque fresco collection. If more culture appeals, hop back on the bus and take in either the **Fundació Joan Miró** (▷ 26–27), on the other side of Montjuïc or the **Museu Marítim** (▷ 24–25), at the foot of the Ramblas, before heading along the waterfront to **Barceloneta** (▷ 62).

Lunch Have lunch with the locals at the **Can Solé** (▷ 77), a great seafood restaurant with a fabulous selection of paellas, fresh fish, lobsters and prawns, before returning to Plaça de Catalunya.

Afternoon Board a red-route bus, which will take you up the Passeig de Gràcia, where you can get off to visit the **Manzana de la Discòrdia** (▷ 86–87), a block containing a trio of compelling *modernista* houses, and then walk north to visit Gaudí's most famous civil building, the **Casa Milà** (▷ 82–83). From here, head east to his most famous creation, the **Sagrada Família** (▷ 90). By 6, the streets around the Passeig de Gràcia will be bustling, and it's a good time for some serious retail therapy.

Dinner Round off your homage to *modernisme* with a late-ish dinner at **Casa Calvet** (▷ 97), an innovative restaurant housed in a Gaudí-designed building.

Evening You could end the day with a couple of hours' partying at **Luz de Gas** (▷ 96), with its variety of live acts, or simply wind down over a late-night drink at a bar.

ESSENTIAL BARCELONA A SHORT STAY IN BARCELONA

Top 25

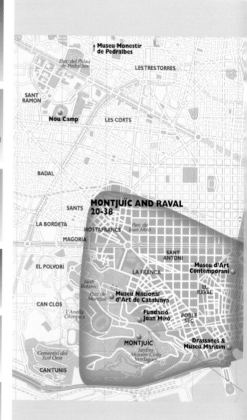

TOP 25

► ► ►

These pages are a quick guide to the Top 25, which are described in more detail later. Here they are listed alphabetically, and the tinted background shows which area they are in.

Catedral ▷ 42–43
Barcelona's great cathedral is a splendid example of Catalan Gothic architecture.

Drassanes and Museu Marítim ▷ 24–25
Discover the city's maritime past in the royal shipyards.

Fundació Joan Miró ▷ 26–27 Iconic modern museum building that showcases work by Miró.

Gràcia ▷ 85 Discover the narrow atmospheric streets and shady squares of the city's bohemian quarter.

Manzana de la Discòrdia ▷ 86–87 Three famous buildings make up the Block of Discord.

Montjuïc ▷ 30 Green and leafy hill, overlooking the port, with a castle and some superb museums.

Museu d'Art Contemporani ▷ 28–29
An ultra-modern art museum at the heart of El Raval.

Museu Monestir de Pedralbes ▷ 102–103
The monastery is an oasis of calm in a busy city.

Museu Nacional d'Art de Catalunya ▷ 31
Collections spanning eight centuries of Catalan art.

Museu Picasso ▷ 63
Showcasing different periods of the artist's work.

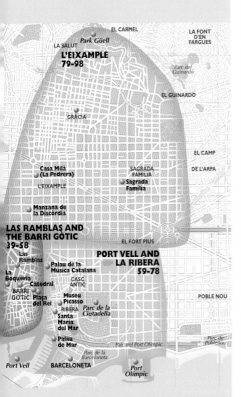

Palau de Mar ▷ 65 This entertaining waterfront museum brings the story of Catalonia to life.

Palau de la Música Catalana ▷ 64 Superb concert hall with a full schedule of classical music.

Nou Camp ▷ 104 Visit the mythical Nou Camp, home to one of the world's most loved football teams.

Shopping

Rich and stylish, as attractive to locals and Spaniards from outside Catalonia as it is to foreigners, the city rates as Spain's number-one shopping destination after Madrid. The contrast between tiny, old-world specialist shops and the glittering bastions of 21st-century retail therapy is striking; shops vary from the ultra-modern to relics from the past.

Leather Goods and Souvenirs

Branches of some of Spain and Europe's best-known fashion sources are here, as well as haunts for urban trendies, which stock classy and coquettish clothes with a twist. Added to that there's a wealth of serious, well-priced leather goods—shoes of every style and shade, bags of all descriptions, and deliciously supple belts, gloves and purses. As for souvenirs of this city of Gaudí, look for useful items with a *modernisme* theme—calendars and art books, vibrant ceramics and porcelain. The textiles are inspired; you can pick up gorgeous throws and fabrics in seductive shades and textures both from specialist shops and workshops.

Designer Bargains

For those who find the temptation of a designer bargain irresistible, a visit to La Roca Company Stores (www.larocavillage.com) will probably be essential. A 30-minute drive from Barcelona are exciting top brands at discounted prices, all in a pretty, 19th-century Catalan village.

Barcelona offers a wealth of fashionable shops, from main street stores to exclusive boutiques

WHERE TO SHOP

Plaça de Catalunya is the place for department store shopping at El Corte Ingles and El Triangle shopping mall, while the Passeig de Gràcia has the big-name stores. You'll find quirky shops throughout the Raval, Gràcia and El Born in the Ribera, Barcelona's hippest 'hood. The Barri Gòtic is great for crafts and antiques; there is a weekend art and bric-a-brac market held outside the port at the southern tip of Las Ramblas and in front of the Cathedral on Thursday. The best flea market is Els Encants at Plaça de la Glories.

Edible Gifts

Edible gifts are always popular; the Spanish specialty, *turrón* (nougat), almonds and olives spring to mind. Head for the Boqueria market and you'll find items such as strings of dried peppers, aromatic honey, golden threads of saffron, sheets of dried cod, superb hams and wonderful cheeses. Spanish nuts and dried fruits are superb, and exciting chocolate boutiques are popping up everywhere.

Crafts and Ceramics

Many craft objects can be picked up for a few euros. Basic beige and yellow ceramics from Catalonia's Costa Brava are inexpensive and plentiful. Reproduction *modernista* tiles are a stunning asset to bathrooms and kitchens. The *alpargatara*, the Catalan espadrille (rope sandal), usually has two-tone ribbons that wrap around the ankle, making stylish summer shoes. Most of these can be picked up in souvenir shops, but they are likely to be mass-produced, so try and seek them out in specialty stores.

Specialist Shops

The old city is the home of Barcelona's best specialist shops. Trawling through the narrow streets of the Barri Gòtic and Raval you'll come across tiny shops devoted to wonderfully esoteric merchandise. There's even a shop devoted entirely to feathers. If you fancy a silk shawl, *mantilla* or intricate fan you'll find it here, as well as deliciously scented candles, flamenco dresses, traditionally made perfumes, soaps and cosmetics.

There are plenty of gift-buying opportunities in Barcelona—specialist food and craft shops abound

THE RAVAL

Along the narrow streets of the Raval, west of Las Ramblas, you will find some of Barcelona's most interesting and one-of-a-kind shops. This is the place to hunt down red-hot design, second-hand fashion, clubwear and dance accessories. Look especially on and around Carrer Riera Baixa, which is home to a Saturday alternative street market, and the Rambla del Raval, which has a market on weekends.

Shopping by Theme

Whether you're looking for a department store, a quirky boutique or something in between, you'll find it all in Barcelona. On this page shops are listed by theme. For a more detailed write-up, see the individual listings in Barcelona by Area.

ARTS, CRAFT AND DESIGN

Alamacen Marabi (▷ 74)
Art Escudellers (▷ 53)
Bagués (▷ 94)
Baraka (▷ 74)
Cereria Subirá (▷ 53)
La Comercial (▷ 74)
Coses de Casa (▷ 53)
Ganivetería (▷ 54)
Iguapop Gallery (▷ 75)
Sala Parés (▷ 54)
Vaho Gallery (▷ 54)
Vinçon (▷ 95)

BOOKS AND MUSIC

Altaïr (▷ 94)
BCN Books (▷ 94)
Castelló (▷ 36)

FASHION

Adolfo DomÍnguez (▷ 94)
Antonio Miro (▷ 94)
Armand Basi (▷ 94)
Como Agua de Mayo (▷ 74)
Custo Barcelona (▷ 36)
Desigual (▷ 94)
Dolores Promesas (▷ 95)
Josep Font (▷ 95)
Mango (▷ 95)
Massimo Dutti (▷ 95)
Menchén Tomás (▷ 75)
On Land (▷ 75)
Santa Eulàlia (▷ 95)
Sephora (▷ 95)

FOOD SHOPS AND MARKETS

Bubó (▷ 74)
Caelum (▷ 53)
Casa Gispert (▷ 74)
Colmado Quilez (▷ 94)
Demasié (▷ 74)
Escribà (▷ 36)
Formatgeria La Seu (▷ 53)
Herboristería del Rei (▷ 54)
Mercat de Santa Caterina (▷ 75)
Olive (▷ 75)
Papabubble (▷ 54)
Vila Viniteca (▷ 75)

GIFTS AND ANTIQUES

Barri Gòtic Antiques Market (▷ 53)
Bulevard dels Antiquaris (▷ 94)
Els Encants Flea Market (▷ 95)
Gidlööf (▷ 74)
El Ingenio (▷ 54)
Ivo & Co (▷ 75)
Joguines Monforte (▷ 54)
Mostra d'Art (▷ 54)
Novedades (▷ 36)
Riera Baixa Secondhand Market (▷ 36)

MALLS AND DEPARTMENT STORES

Bulevard Rosa (▷ 94)
El Corte Inglés (▷ 53)
L'Illa (▷ 95)
Maremagnum (▷ 75)
El Triangle (▷ 54)

SHOES AND ACCESSORIES

Alamacenes de Pilar (▷ 53)
Beatriz Furest (▷ 74)
Camper (▷ 94)
Da Vinci Colors (▷ 53)
La Manual Alpargatera (▷ 54)
Minu Madhu (▷ 75)
Tous (▷ 95)
Vialis (▷ 36)

Barcelona by Night

Las Ramblas (▷ 46–47), the perfect place to stroll, pause and relax, acts like a magnet for an evening *paseo*. Amble up and down its length a couple of times, then grab a table at one of the many cafés and watch the world go by. Alternatively, start at the somewhat seedily elegant Plaça Reial (▷ 51) nearby. Other pleasant areas to stroll include the waterfront and Port Vell (▷ 68–69) and the Eixample for its wide boulevards, most notably the Passeig de Gràcia and Rambla Catalunya. The streets of the Barri Gòtic are also atmospheric.

Music, Theatre, Dance and Film

Barcelona has a good schedule of cultural evening events. The choice is wide, with everything from opera, orchestral concerts, plays and original language films to jazz, flamenco and Latin American music. You can get information in the weekly entertainment guide *Guia del Ocio* and from the Virreina Cultural Information Centre on the Rambla (tel 93 316 10 00), or call the 010 information line, where an English-speaking operator will help.

Clubbing the Night Away

Barcelona is a clubber's paradise, with frequent visits from internationally famous DJs, plenty of homegrown talent and a constantly evolving scene. Clubs and bars open and close frequently so pick up flyers and check the listings in *Barcelona Metropolitan* and *Guia del Ocio.*

Barcelona's diverse nightlife includes some of Europe's top venues, clubs and bars

ESSENTIAL BARCELONA   BARCELONA BY NIGHT

PICK OF THE PANORAMAS

From the slopes of Tibidabo, the huge peak towering behind the city, there are views over the whole city to the sea, and the area is scattered with a few bars and cafés. The mountain's name comes from the Latin *tibi dabo*—'to thee I give', the words used by the Devil when tempting Christ. Another great view can be had from Montjüic, where there are green spaces to enjoy on summer evenings. Take the *teleféric* up to the castle for a bird's-eye view over the hill and the port below.

Eating Out

Eating out in this city is a pleasure, with the emphasis firmly on seasonal and fresh produce, and a huge range of restaurants, snack bars, tapas bars, cafés and *granjas* feeding residents and visitors day and night.

Breakfast
If you're staying in a hotel, check if breakfast is included in the price. If not, join locals in a bar for a *café con leche* (milky coffee) and croissant or *flauta* (breadstick stuffed with cheese or ham). Fresh orange juice is available but butter for your toast (*tostadas*) isn't, you'll be handed a bottle of olive oil instead. For something more substantial, try a *tortilla francesa* (omelette) or *bikini* (toasted ham and cheese sandwich).

Lunch
Lunch is the main meal, and most eat a fixed-price *menu del migdía* in a restaurant. You may get something light such as *escalivada* (roast peppers and aubergine) or a soup for starters, followed by grilled fish or meat or a rice dish (these rarely come with vegetables). Desserts are simple; fresh fruit or yogurt or a *crema catalana* (crème brûlée). A glass of wine or bottled water is included in the price.

Dinner
Dinner is generally a lighter meal and many locals just go for the ubiquitous *pa amb tomàquet* (rustic bread rubbed with tomato pulp) topped with cheese or charcuterie or make a meal out of tapas. Freshly grilled squid, prawns or baked cod are also popular choices.

RESERVATIONS

Booking is advised in mid- to upper-price restaurants, particularly for groups of four or more and on the weekends. For less formal places, such as tapas bars, you can walk in and secure a table, even if you have to wait at the bar for a space to become available. However, if there is an establishment you really want to visit, check out whether booking is necessary.

There is a huge variety of restaurants and cafés at which to enjoy Barcelona's wonderful local produce

Restaurants by Cuisine

There are restaurants to suit all tastes and budgets in Barcelona. On this page they are listed by cuisine. For a more detailed description of each restaurant, see Barcelona by Area.

BODEGAS, CAFÉS AND TAPAS BARS

Bar del Pí (▷ 57)
La Bodega de Palma (▷ 57)
La Bombeta (▷ 77)
Cacao Sampaka (▷ 97)
Café de l'Opera (▷ 57)
Cerveceria Catalana (▷ 97)
Ciudad Condal (▷ 98)
Cornelia & Co (▷ 98)
Mam i Teca (▷ 38)
Paco Meralgo (▷ 98)
Quimet & Quimet (▷ 38)
Taller de Tapas (▷ 58)
Tickets Bar (▷ 38)
Vinateria del Call (▷ 58)

CATALAN

Agut (▷ 57)
Alkimia (▷ 97)
Can Culleretes (▷ 57)
Casa Calvet (▷ 97)
Casa Delfín (▷ 77)
Comerç 24 (▷ 78)
La Cuina del Do (▷ 57)
Embat (▷ 98)

Jaume de Provença (▷ 98)
L'Olivé (▷ 98)
Els Quatre Gats (▷ 58)
Set Portes (▷ 78)

INTERNATIONAL

Atril (▷ 77)
Bestial (▷ 77)
Café de l'Academia (▷ 57)
Chido One (▷ 97)
Cinc Sentits (▷ 97)
Ikibana (▷ 98)
Koy Shunka (▷ 58)
Little Italy (▷ 78)
Peimong (▷ 58)
Pla (▷ 58)

MEDITERRANEAN

Ánima (▷ 38)
Basilico (▷ 38)
Bosco (▷ 57)
Carmelitas (▷ 38)
Lia d'en Vicius (▷ 38)
El Magatzem del Port (▷ 78)

NOUVELLE CUISINE

Moo (▷ 98)

REGIONAL SPANISH

Agua (▷ 77)
El Asador de Burgos (▷ 97)
Botafumeiro (▷ 97)
Centre Cultural Euskal Etxea (▷ 77)
Las Fernandez (▷ 38)
Mesón David (▷ 38)

SEAFOOD

El Cangrejo Loco (▷ 77)
Can Solé (▷ 77)
Kaiku (▷ 78)
La Paradeta (▷ 78)

VEGETARIAN

Juicy Jones (▷ 58)

A friendly welcome at a Barcelonan restaurant

If You Like...

However you'd like to spend your time in Barcelona, these top suggestions should help you tailor your ideal visit. Each suggestion has a fuller write-up elsewhere in the book.

A LAZY MORNING

Stroll down Las Ramblas (▷ 46–47) and take in the flower stalls and street entertainment.
Relax over a drink in the faded grandeur of the Plaça Reial (▷ 51).
Enjoy the cool greenery, lake and fountains in the Parc de la Ciutadella (▷ 66).

WATERSIDE LIFE

Head for the Port Vell (▷ 68–69) for craft stalls, walkways and cafés in a glorious seafront setting.
Take a harbour trip in the *golondrinas* (▷ 68).
Visit the Aquàrium to discover what's under the sea (▷ 69).

Mercat de la Boqueria (above), a shop in the Ribera (below) and Parc de la Ciutadella (bottom)

A TOUCH OF RETAIL THERAPY

Stroll the Passeig de Gràcia (▷ panel 94) for credit-card stretching luxury boutiques.
Trawl the narrow streets of the Barri Gòtic (▷ 49), the Raval (▷ 35) and the Ribera (▷ 73) for some of the city's most original stores.
Hit the Boqueria market on the Ramblas (▷ 48) for a spread of food stalls that's among the best in the Med.

VISITING THE CULTURE TRAIL

Trace the artistic development of one of the world's foremost 20th-century creators at the Museu Picasso (▷ 63).
Explore the Barri Gòtic (▷ 52) with its ancient cathedral and museums.
Let the vibrant pictures and sculptures in the Fundació Joan Miró fill you in on the spirit of Barcelona (▷ 26–27).

A cablecar view of the port (below) and the Parc de la Ciutadella (below middle)

MOVING WITH STYLE

For a taste of the past, take a horse-drawn carriage round the Ramblas and waterfront.

Take a harbour cruise on one of the charmingly old-fashioned double-decker *golondrinas* (swallowboats; ▷ 69).

Hire a bike from any one of the dozens of outlets or at the tourist offices.

CITY PANORAMAS

Take the elevator to the cathedral roof for a bird's-eye view of the Barri Gòtic (▷ 42–43).

See all Barcelona spread at your feet from the top of the Torre de Collserola on Tibidabo (▷ 106).

For ever-changing city views, stroll through the landscaped greenery of Montjuïc (▷ 30).

Soar high above the port area by the cablecar that runs from Barceloneta to Montjuïc.

A classic Catalan salad (above) and the Bestial restaurant by night (below)

ROMANTIC RESTAURANTS

Enjoy the best of Catalan traditional cuisine in the 18th-century surroundings of Can Culleretes (▷ 57), where a series of rambling rooms is decorated with oil paintings and signed photos.

Relax under a parasol on the decking of Bestial and watch the sea while you eat Italian-style (▷ 77).

Soak up the atmosphere while you enjoy old-fashioned service and surroundings par excellence at the Set Portes (▷ 78).

Spend an evening dining in a Gaudí building at the Casa Calvet (▷ 97).

MODERNISME

See it in all its variations by taking in the Manzana de la Discòrdia on Passeig de Gràcia—three different houses by the biggest names in *modernista* architecture (▷ 86–87).

Gaudí mosaic in Park Güell (below) and the beach at Barceloneta (below middle)

Relax in a sumptuous interior at the Palau de la Música Catalana (▷ 64), where *modernista* decorative arts and music come together.

Take in *modernisme's* most iconic emblem, Gaudí's Sagrada Família (▷ 90–91).

FRESH AIR AND GREEN SPACES

Combine fresh air and green space with *modernista* buildings and mosaics in the Park Güell (▷ 88–89).

Take the kids to Montjuïc for grass, plants and trees in downtown Barcelona (▷ 30).

SOMETHING FOR NOTHING

Entertainment in the shape of street performers is free to everyone along the Ramblas (▷ 46–47).

Sunbathing and swimming on Barcelona's beaches is a great way to have a free day out (▷ 67).

Take advantage of free Sunday afternoon entry in some of Barcelona's top museums, including the Museu Picasso (▷ 63).

A street entertainer in the Ramblas (above)

ENTERTAINING YOUR KIDS

Kids can let off steam on bikes and skates or visit the Zoo Barcelona in the Parc de la Ciutadella (▷ 66).

The Aquàrium and the IMAX cinema at the Port Vell are top of the list for many young visitors (▷ 68–69).

The Aquàrium at the Port Vell (right)

Barcelona by Area

The hill of Montjuïc combines its role as a recreational area and a cultural stronghold with style, drawing in thousands of visitors. It overlooks the Raval, which underwent a major clean-up in the 1990s.

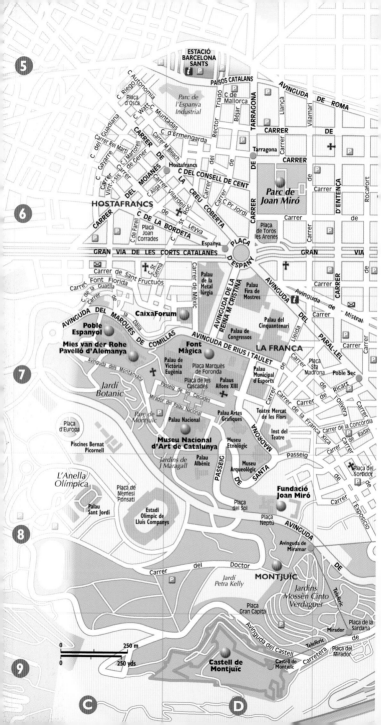

5

6

7

8

9

ESTACIÓ
BARCELONA
SANTS

C. Autonomia
C. Riego
Plaça
d'Osca
Watt
C. Muntades
C. d'Ermengarda
C. M Bleach
Hostafrancs

PAISOS CATALANS

Triadó
C de Mallorca
Béjar

AVINGUDA DE ROMA

Lançà
Vilamari

Parc de
l'Espanya
Industrial

CARRER
DE

TARRAGONA

Tarragona

CARRER

DE

D'ENTENÇA

Rocafort

Carrer del Rei Martí
C. Callao
C. Vint. Isis
C. Cavaire
Carrer
Guadiana
CARRER
DEL
MOIANES

C. del Gener
C. C. Martorell
Carrer
Vilardell
de

C DEL CONSELL DE CENT

Parc de
Joan Miró

HOSTAFRANCS

C. de Farell
Plaça
Joan
Corrades

CARRER
C DE LA BORDETA

Espanya

Sts. Leyva

LA
CREU
COBERTA

C Pr Jordi

PLAÇA
D'ESPANY

Plaça
de Toros
les Arenes

Carrer

GRAN VIA DE LES CORTS CATALANES

Carrer de Sant Fructuós
Font
Florida
C. de la Guatlla
Carrer de Mèxic

Palau
de la
Metal
lúrgia

AVINGUDA DE LA REINA M CRISTINA

Palau
Fira de
Mostres

GRAN VIA

CARRER

Mistral

AVINGUDA DEL PARAL·LEL

CaixaForum

AVINGUDA DEL MARQUES DE COMILLAS

Palau del
Cinquantenari

Poble
Espanyol

Dàlia

Palau de
Congressos

Lleida

Mies van der Rohe
Pavelló d'Alemanya

Font
Màgica

AVINGUDA DE RIUS I TAULET

LA FRANCA

Plaça
Sta
Madrona

Poble Sec

Avinguda dels Montanyans

Palau de
Victòria
Eugènia

Plaça Marquès
de Foronda

Palau
Municipal
d'Esports

Ricart

Jardí
Botànic

Passeig de les cascades

Plaça de les
Cascades

Palaus
Alfons XIII

Carrer de la Franca Xica

Olivera

Mirador del Palau Nacional

Parc de
Montjuïc

Palau Nacional

Palau Artes
Grafiques

Teatre Mercat
de les Flors

Carrer de la Concordia

Radas

Plaça
d'Europa

Piscines Bernat
Picornell

Jardins de
J Maragall

Museu Nacional
d'Art de Catalunya

Palau
Albéniz

Museu
Etnològic

PASSEIG

Inst del
Teatre

passeig

Plaça del
Sortidor

d'Exposició

L'Anella
Olímpica

Plaça de
Nemesi
Ponsati

Estadi
Olímpic de
Lluís Companys

Museu
Arqueològic

DE
SANTA

Fundació
Joan Miró

Carrer

Palau
Sant Jordi

Plaça
del Sol

Plaça
Neptú

AVINGUDA

MONTJUÏC

DE

Avinguda de
Miramar

Carrer
del
Doctor

Jardí
Petra Kelly

Jardins
Mossèn Cinto
Verdaguer

Teleferic

Mirador

Plaça
Gran Capità

Plaça de la
Sardana

AVINGUDA del Castell

Teleferic

de

Plaça del
Mirador

0   250 m
0   250 yds

Castell de
Montjuïc

Castell de
Montjuïc

Carretera

C

D

VALÈNCIA

D'ARAGÓ

del

VILADOMAT

Consell

de

D'URGELL

Cent

Villarroel

CARRER DE CASANOVA

DE MUNTANER

CARRER D'ARIBAU

Calabria

la

Diputació

Borrell

COMTE

Universitat
Central

Rocafort

DE

LES

CORTS

CATALANES

Urgell

DEL

PLAÇA DE LA
UNIVERSITAT

SANT
ANTONI

de

Comte

Sepúlveda

Plaça
Goya

Plaça
de
Castella

de

DE

CARRER

Fioridablanca

DE

SANT

ANTONI

Costa

Joaquin

Valldoncella

Carrer

C de Tigre

Carrer de la
Paloma

Centre de Cultura
Contemporania
de Barcelona

de

Tamarit

Museu d'Art
Contemporani

de

Sant
Antoni

RONDA

C de la Riera

Foment de les
Arts Decoratives

Carrer de

Manso

Alta

Carrer
del Peu

Carrer
de la Creu

C dels Àngels

Carrer

de

CARRER

Parlament

EL
RAVAL

CARRER

DEL

CARME

AVINGUDA

CARRER

C del Marquès
de Campo Sagrado

CARRER DE L'HOSPITAL

Antic
Hospital
Santa Creu

Santa
Madrona

DE

Carrer

Carrer

Rafael

d'Elkano

Margarit

SANT

Carrer
Aldana

de les

Carretes

de

la Riereta

Rambla del Raval

Carrer Robadòr

Carrer Junta de Com

Carrer

de

Tapioles

Poeta

Cabanyes

RONDA

Sant

Pau

Magallanes

Carrer

salva

POBLE
SEC

PARAL-LEL

Carrer del Roser

Carrer

de

C del Marquès de
Barbera

Carrer

Nou

de

la

Rambla

Sant Pau
del Camp

Carrer Nou de la Rambla

Carrer

de Lafont

Paral-lel

C de l'Om

DEL

C de l'Arc

del Teatre

Passeig

de

Passeig

Carrer

de

Cabanes

Vila

i

Piquer

del Cid

de les Drassanes

C de l'Arc Bisbal

MIRAMAR

Carrer

de

Plaça
Carles
Ibañez

Carrer
Palaudàries

Montjuïc

Carrer Puig IX

Drassanes &
Museu Marítim

Montjuïc

Miramar

Jardins de
Miramar

PLAÇA DE LES
DRASSANES

CARNER

Jardins del
Josep Costa
i Llobera

PASSEIG

DE

JOSEP

RONDA

LITORAL

ESTACIÓ
MARÍTIMA

E   F   G

Drassanes and Museu Marítim

HIGHLIGHTS

● Medieval navigation charts
● Displays on 19th-century submarine *Ictíneo*
● Figurehead collection
● Fishing caravel of 1907

TIP

● Come in the afternoon to avoid the school parties.

Cut off from today's port by cobbled docksides, the Gothic buildings of the Royal Shipyards are an evocative reminder of Barcelona's long-standing affair with the sea, as well as a unique monument to the Middle Ages.

Cathedral of the sea By the 13th century, Catalan sea power extended over much of the western Mediterranean. Ships were built in the covered Royal Shipyards, or Drassanes, a series of parallel halls with roofs supported on high arches. The effect is of sheer grandeur—of a cathedral rather than a functional workspace.

Ships on show The Drassanes are now a fascinating museum, displaying paintings, charts, model ships, a number of boats as well as

The *Galera Real is one of the finest boats on display in the museum (left and right), and includes some superbly detailed artwork (bottom right)*

maritime memorabilia. These are all upstaged by the *Galera Real*, a full-size reproduction of the galley from which Don Juan d'Austria oversaw the defeat of the Turkish navy at the Battle of Lepanto in 1571. Built to commemorate the 400th anniversary of the battle, this elegant vessel is nearly 20m (65ft) long. The original was propelled to victory at high speed by chained galley slaves. You can see statues of some of them, along with the commander who stands in the ornate stern, from a high catwalk, which also gives you a view of the building itself.

Museum redesign The museum is being remodelled, and is just showing temporary exhibitions. You can visit the *Santa Eulàlia*, an early 20th-century clipper, which is in the Port Vell and forms part of the Museu Marítim's collection.

THE BASICS

www.mmb.cat
+ F8
✉ Avinguda de les Drassanes s/n
☎ 93 342 99 20
🕐 Daily 10–8. Closed 1 Jan, 6 Jan, 25–26 Dec. *Santa Eulàlia*: Apr–Oct Tue–Fri, Sun 10–8.30, Sat 2–8.30pm; Nov–Feb Tue–Fri, Sun 10–5.30, Sat 2–5.30pm
🚇 Drassanes
🚌 14, 36, 38, 57, 59, 64, 91
♿ Few
💷 Moderate; free Sun after 3pm

Fundació Joan Miró

Poised on the flank of Montjuïc is this white-walled temple to the art of Joan Miró; its calm interior spaces, patios and terraces are an ideal setting for the works of this most Catalan of all artists.

Miró and Barcelona Born in Barcelona in 1893, Joan Miró never lost his feeling for the city and the surrounding countryside, though he spent much of the 1920s and 1930s in Paris and Mallorca. His paintings and sculptures, with their intense primary colours and swelling, dancing and wriggling forms, are instantly recognizable, but he also gained renown for his expressive ceramics and graphic drawings inspired by political turmoil in Spain. Miró's distinctive influence is visible in graphic work all over Barcelona and locals as well as tourists flock to the Foundation, which is also a cultural

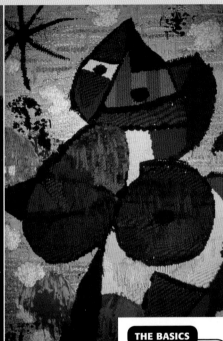

Alexander Calder's Quatre ailes (Four Wings) *(1972) in the grounds of the Fundació Joan Miró (left); 10,000 of Miró's works are on display, including this vibrant woven tapestry (right)*

hub dedicated to the promotion of contemporary art. It houses changing exhibitions, concerts, a library, shops and a café. Miró's works (11,000 in all, including 240 paintings) are complemented by those of numerous contemporaries including Balthus, Calder, Duchamp, Ernst, Léger, Matisse and Moore.

Mediterranean masterpiece The monumental yet intimate Foundation was built in 1974 by Miró's friend and collaborator, the architect Josep-Luis Sert, in a style that remains modern, yet traditionally Mediterranean in its use of forms such as domes, arches, and roof and terracotta floor tiles. It sits easily in the landscape, and its interpenetrating spaces incorporate old trees like the ancient olive in one of the courtyards. There are glorious views over the city, especially from the roof terrace.

THE BASICS

www.fundaciomiro-bcn.org

✚ D8

✉ Parc de Montjuïc

☎ 93 443 94 70

🕐 Jul–Sep Tue–Sat 10–8 (Thu 10–9.30), Sun and hols 10–2.30; Oct–Jun Tue–Sat 10–7 (Thu 10–9.30), Sun and hols 10–2.30. Closed 1 Jan, 25–26 Dec

🍴 Café-restaurant

🚇 Espanya

🚌 50, 55

🚠 Montjuïc funicular from Paral·lel Metro

♿ Good

💶 Expensive

❓ Book and gift shop

Museu d'Art Contemporani

TOP
25

HIGHLIGHTS

Works in the collection (not necessarily on show) by
- Miquel Barceló
- Jean-Michel Basquiat
- Joseph Beuys
- Antoni Clavé
- Xavier Grau
- Richard Long
- Robert Rauschenberg
- Antoni Tàpies

TIP

● The excellent bookshop has a wide selection, including exhibition catalogues from past shows, designer classics and accessories.

Could this be Barcelona's answer to Paris's Centre Pompidou? A glittering white home for late 20th-century art, known as the MACBA, has given the run-down inner city district of Raval an ultra-modern shot in the arm.

A modern museum For many years Barcelona felt the lack of an adequate establishment devoted to the contemporary visual arts. During the repressive Franco years, its progressive artists enjoyed little official encouragement. Now two major institutions are bringing it back into the mainstream. By any reckoning, the Museum of Contemporary Art is remarkable, though its long white walls and huge size are strikingly at odds with the ramshackle facades of the surrounding buildings across the wide modern *plaça* in an up and coming part

The spectacular Richard Meier-designed Museu d'Art Contemporani de Barcelona was opened in 1995

of town. The shining structure, designed by the American architect Richard Meier, opened in 1995. Its exhibition spaces lead to a great atrium and are reached by a spectacular series of ramps and glass-floored galleries, sometimes almost upstaging the works on display. Temporary exhibitions featuring local and international artists complement the museum's own extensive collection, which is exhibited in rotation.

Centre de Cultura Contemporània Housed adjacent in the striking old poor house buildings of the Casa de la Caritat, the Centre for Contemporary Culture promotes a range of activities focused on cultural and social themes. Each year sees a season of cultural and theatrical events exploring different aspects of contemporary art and style, from fashion and architecture to modern communications.

THE BASICS

www.macba.cat

⊕ F7

✉ Museum, Plaça dels Àngels 1; CCCB, Montalegre 5

☎ Museum: 93 412 08 10; CCCB: 93 306 41 00

🕐 MACBA: 25 Sep–23 Jun Mon, Wed–Fri 11–7.30, Sat 10–8, Sun and hols 10–3; 24 Jun–24 Sep Mon, Wed–Fri 11–8 (Thu, Fri until midnight), Sun and hols 10–3. CCCB: Tue–Sun 11–8 (Thu until 10)

🚇 Catalunya, Universitat

🚌 9, 14, 24, 38, 41, 50, 54, 55, 58, 59, 66, 91 and all routes to Plaça Catalunya

♿ Good

💶 Moderate; CCCB free 1st Wed each month, Thu 8–10 and Sun 3–8

29

Montjuïc

The Palau Sant Jordi stadium (left) and the Plaça Sardana (right)

THE BASICS

✚ B8/9, C7/8/9, D7/8/9, E8/9

🍴 Restaurants and cafés

🚇 Espanya, Paral·lel (then funicular)

🚌 61, 50, 55

❓ Telefèric (cablecar) to the upper peaks

HIGHLIGHTS

Buildings and structures
● Fundació Joan Miró (▷ 26–27)
● Magic fountains (Plaça Carlos Buigas)
● The castle for its fabulous views

Gardens
● Parc Joan Brossa
● Mossen Costa I Llobera gardens
● Jardí Botànic
● Teatre Grec amphitheatre

Covering an area bigger than the Barri Gòtic, 'Jove's mountain' rises imposingly over the port. This is the city's finest park, a unique blend of exotic gardens and tourist attractions, including two of the city's finest museums.

Ancient beginnings Prehistoric people had settled here, high above the bay, long before the Romans built their shrine to Jove, and the hill's quarries were the source of stone from which half the old city was built. Montjuïc has also always been a place of burial, represented today in the Cimentiri del Sud-Oest on the hill's far flank. Crowning the summit is the 17th-century castle-fort, which you are free to roam around (▷ 32).

The 1929 Expo Montjuïc really came into its own in the 20th century. The Expo was preceded by a long period of preparation in which the slopes were terraced and planted to create the luxuriant landscape that exists today. Exhibition buildings were put up in a variety of styles ranging from the pompous Palau Nacional (▷ 31) to one of the key works of modern architecture, the Germany Pavilion by Mies van der Rohe (▷ 34). One of the Expo's main attractions was the Poble Espanyol (▷ 34) and the great City Stadium was second only to London's Wembley in size. When the Olympic Games came to Barcelona in 1992, Montjuïc became Mount Olympus; the Anella Olímpica (Olympic Ring) includes the splendidly restored stadium as well as the close-by flying-saucer-like Palau Sant Jordi.

The Palau Nacional provides a superb setting for the collection of Catalan art

Museu Nacional d'Art de Catalunya

The Palau Nacional dominates the north flank of Montjuïc and houses the National Museum of Catalan Art. Its mural paintings, sculptures, frescoes, woodcarvings and pictures offer a staggering complete overview of a millennium of Catalan art.

Romanesque riches The entire west wing of the ground floor concentrates on the museum's major treasure, the mural paintings rescued from isolated 10th-century churches high in the Pyrenees. This exceptionally rich heritage of Romanesque art was created as Christianity recolonized the mountain valleys during the 12th and 13th centuries. Powerful images of Christ in Majesty, the Virgin Mary and the saints promoted piety among a peasant population recently released from the Moorish yoke. By the early 20th century, such art enjoyed little prestige and it was only through the heroic efforts of a dedicated band of art historians and archaeologists that so much was saved from decay and theft. There are 21 mural sections, loosely arranged in chronological order.

Medieval to Modernism Elsewhere in the museum the rooms are given over to a rich collection of Gothic art thanks to two important bequests. The Thyssen-Bornemisza and the Cambó collections include works from El Greco, Tintoretto, Titian and Rubens. Upstairs the MNAC holds a dazzling collection of *modernista* painting, furniture and decorative arts, much of it taken from the stately homes of the Eixample and including some fluid furniture from Gaudí.

THE BASICS

www.mnac.cat
+ D7
✉ Palau Nacional, Parc de Montjuïc
☎ 936 22 03 76
🕐 Tue–Sat 10–8 (10–6 Oct–Apr), Sun 10–3. Closed 1 Jan, 1 May, 25 Dec
🚇 Espanya
🚌 13, 37, 50, 55, 57 and all buses to Plaça Espanya
♿ Good
💶 Moderate; free 1st Sun of month

HIGHLIGHTS

● Apse de Santa Maria de Taüll (Ambit V)
● Aragonese Chapter House Paintings (Ambit XI)
● *The retables* by Jaume Huguet (Ambit XIII)
● *Virgin de la Humilidad* by Fra Angélico (Ambit 48)
● *San Pedro y San Pablo* by El Greco (Ambit 42)
● Roman Casas y Pere Romeu en un tandem (Ambit 71)
● *Grandina* by Hermana Anglada Camarasa (Ambit 77)

More to See

CAIXAFORUM

www.fundacio.lacaixa.es

A stunning conversion of a *modernista* textile factory, funded by La Caixa, Catalonia's largest savings bank. Its revamp gave it an entrance plaza, auditorium, library and some impressive exhibition space. In addition to the permanent collection, major international temporary exhibitions are staged throughout the year; previous years have included shows devoted to architect Richard Rogers and Islamic Art.
⊞ D7 ✉ Casaramona, Avinguda del Marquès de Comillas 6–8 ☎ 93 476 86 00 🕐 Daily 10–8 (Sat until 10) 🚇 Espanya 🎟 Free

CASTELL DE MONTJUÏC

The impressive fort-castle facing the sea on Montjuïc has had a dark history since it was built in the 17th century by the Spanish government to ensure that the rebellious Catalans remained under control. Long used as a prison and place of execution, it was here that Lluís Companys, president of Catalonia, was shot in 1940 at the end of the Spanish Civil War. It is now being remodelled to contain a Peace Centre. In the meantime, visitors are free to wander around and enjoy the views. The castle hosts an outdoor cinema during the summer.
⊞ D9 ✉ Carretera de Montjuïc 66 ☎ 93 256 44 45 🕐 Oct–Mar Tue–Sun 9–7; Nov–Feb Tue–Sun 9–9 🚌 Montjuïc Turístic, Telefèric de Montjuïc, PM Bus

FONT MÀGICA

Barcelona's 'magic fountain' is one of its most pleasing attractions. A relic of the 1929 international exhibition at the base of the stairs to the MNAC (▷ 31), the ornamental fountain looks like any other during the day. But come nightfall it comes to life with a spectacular light-and-music show—the water spurts 'dance' to the beats, while a rainbow of tinted lights add a Las Vegas-type neon glow to the water. Arrive early to get a seat at one of the outdoor cafés or limited public seating.
⊞ D7 ✉ Plaça Buïgas 1 🕐 Apr–Sep Thu–Sun 9pm–11.30pm; Oct–Mar Fri–Sat 7pm–9pm 🚇 Espanya 🎟 Free

Inside the Olympic Stadium (▷ 30); Mies van der Rohe Pavelló statue (right, ▷ 34)

MIES VAN DER ROHE PAVELLÓ D'ALEMANYA

www.miesbcn.com

Germany's contribution to the Expo of 1929 was this supremely cool construction of steel, glass and marble that reinvented all the rules of architecture. It has become an icon of modern (as opposed to *modernista*) design. Yet amazingly, the building was demolished when the fair was over. It was rebuilt by devoted admirers in the mid-1980s and is now a compulsory stop for architecture students.

✚ C7 ✉ Pavelló Barcelona, Avinguda del Marquès de Comillas ☎ 93 423 40 16 🕐 Daily 10–8 🚇 Espanya 💷 Moderate

PARC DE JOAN MIRÓ (PARC DE L'ESCORXADOR)

The sculptor's giant polychromatic *Woman and Bird* dominates this park with its orderly rows of palm trees. It is laid out on the site of an old slaughter-house, l'Escorxador, where bulls were taken after fights.

✚ D6 ✉ Carrer de Tarragona 🕐 Open access 🍴 Cafés 🚇 Tarragona, Espanya

POBLE ESPANYOL

www.poble-espanyol.com

Barcelona's 'Spanish Village' provides a whistle-stop tour of the country's architecture and urban scenery. Craft shops, cafés and restaurants and a new museum add to the appeal.

✚ C7 ✉ Avinguda Marquès de Comillas s/n ☎ 93 508 63 00 🕐 Sun 9am–midnight, Mon 9–8, Fri–Sat 9am–4am, Tue–Thu 9am–2am (shops close around 6–8pm; restaurants much later) 🚇 Espanya 🚌 13, 50, 61 and all routes to Plaça Espanya 💷 Moderate

SANT PAU DEL CAMP

This village church was in the middle of the countryside when it was built in the 12th century. It replaced an older building, probably dating from Visigothic times, which was wrecked by Moorish invaders. The highlight is the miniature cloister, flanked by elegantly carved columns. The facade's simple and severe sculptural decoration includes the symbols of the Evangelists and the Hand of God.

✚ F8 ✉ Carrer de Sant Pau 101 🕐 Mon–Sun 10–1.30, 4–7.30 🚇 Paral·lel

Poble Espanyol

Sculpture at the Parc de Joan Miró

A Walk
Through El Raval

This walk gives a good chance to experience the atmosphere of this teeming and historic multi-ethnic working area.

DISTANCE: 2km (1.2 miles) **ALLOW:** 45–50 minutes

START

BOQUERIA MARKET
🔲 G7 ▷ 48 🔲 Liceu

1 With the Boqueria on your right walk south for about 50m (55 yards) and take the first right into Carrer de l'Hospital. Walk along here, passing Plaça Sant Agustí on your left, until you come to the Gothic complex of the Antic Hospital on your right.

2 After visiting the inner courtyard, exit and turn right. Continue to the Rambla de Raval, a tree-lined promenade with cafés and an outdoor market on weekends. Turn right. Halfway down on the left is the new cylinder-shaped Barceló Raval hotel and opposite, the *Gat* (cat) sculpture by Colombian Fernando Botero.

3 At the bottom turn right on Carrer de Sant Pau, which crosses the bottom end of the Rambla de Raval. Cross the Rambla and continue along Carrer de Sant Pau to the beautiful church of Sant Pau del Camp.

END

RONDA DE SANT ANTONI
🔲 F6 🔲 Universitat

8 Continue to the end of Carrer de Joaquin Costa and turn right onto the Ronda de Sant Antoni.

7 Continue uphill over a crossroads and after 200m (220 yards) you will see a pedestrianized street leading to the MACBA (▷ 28–29) on your right.

6 After 50m (55 yards), in a tiny *plaça* with a column topped by a statue of the Virgin, take the left-hand fork. Where the road widens keep the bright facade of the *farmacia* on your left and take the next left turn onto Carrer Joaquin Costa.

5 Take the first left and continue to a T-junction with Carrer de Sant Antoni Abat. Turn right.

4 Leave the church and cross the street diagonally left to take a right turn into Carrer de la Reina Amàlia. Walk all the way along here, passing one crossroads, to the next where you turn right onto Carrer de la Cera.

Shopping

CASTELLÓ

One of Barcelona's oldest record shops, Castello stocks a range of styles, including pop, folk, world and classical music.

➕ G8 ✉ Tallers 7 ☎ 93 302 59 46 🚇 Liceu

CUSTO BARCELONA

The Custo brothers' bright and funky T-shirts are now worn by trendsetters across the world from Toronto to Tokyo, but their hometown store has the best selection.

➕ G7 ✉ Las Ramblas 109 ☎ 93 481 39 30 🚇 Liceu

ESCRIBÀ

Barcelona's finest *chocolateria* is housed in a lovely *modernista* building right on the Ramblas. Stop here for melt-in-the-mouth chocolates, cakes and to admire the extravagant chocolate creations.

➕ G8 ✉ Las Ramblas 83 ☎ 93 301 60 27 🚇 Liceu

NOVEDADES

For a unique gift or souvenir, take in a photo of the loved one you left behind and the nimble fingers of Lolitas will make up a cute, cartoon-faced, rag doll in their likeness. Other items in the range include animal brooches and T-shirts.

➕ F7 ✉ Carrer Peu de la Creu 24 ☎ 93 329 16 36 🚇 Liceu

RIERA BAIXA SECOND -HAND MARKET

A pretty, pedestrianized street filled with retro boutiques, flea-market stores, costume houses and knick-knack emporiums. Visit on Saturday afternoon when the stores spill on to the pavement and vintage bargains abound.

➕ G8 ✉ Carrer Riera Baixa 🚇 Sant Antoni

VIALIS

Beautiful handmade shoes from Mallorca combine artisan methods with hip design, and have quickly become the footwear of choice for trendy Barceloneses.

➕ G7 ✉ Carrer Elisabets 20 ☎ 93 342 60 71 🚇 Liceu

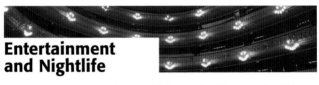

Entertainment and Nightlife

BAR ALMIRALL

This atmospheric *fin de siècle* bar is famous for *absenta*, the supposedly hallucinogenic liquor preferred by 19th-century bohemians, though most locals settle into the cracked leather sofas with a glass of good whisky.

➕ G7 ✉ Carrer Joaquim Costa 33 ☎ No phone 🚇 Universitat

BAR ULTRAMARINOS

Famous for its gin and tonics prepared with a dizzying choice of gins,

this friendly little cocktail bar also features a wide range of other drinks including nightly specials. With its relaxed, arty vibe, it's a great place to start the night.

➕ E8 ✉ Carrer Sant Pau 36 ☎ 65 358 24 24 🕐 Daily 8pm–2am 🚇 Paral·lel

BODEGA 1800

This charming, tiny hole-in-the-wall offers wine and vermouth by the glass and a selection of aperitif-type *tapas*, such as olives and anchovies.

There are a few tables inside and out, but be prepared for standing room only.

➕ G7 ✉ Carrer del Carme 31 ☎ 93 317 30 79 🕐 Closed Sun, Mon 🚇 Liceu

LAS GUINDAS

This narrow, swinging sixties-inspired bar has local funk and soul aficionados taking turns to share their collection with a young and groovy crowd. There's no dance floor, so do your thing at the bar.

➕ F8 ✉ Carrer de San

Pau 126 ☎ 670 437 709
🚇 Paral·lel

JAZZ SÍ CLUB
The bar belonging to
the local music school
offers live music nightly.
Most gigs start around
7.30 (check the door for
details) and the night
denotes the genre, from
blues, rock and jazz to flamenco and jam sessions.
The reasonable cover
charge includes a drink.
🟩 F7 ✉ Carrer
Requesens 2 ☎ 93 329
00 20 🕐 Closed Mon
🚇 Universitat, Sant Antoni

LONDON BAR
Here since 1910, this former bohemian bar, later
taken up by local hippies,
now draws a cosmo-
politan mix of locals and
young foreign residents.
🟩 G8 ✉ Carrer Nou de la
Rambla 34 ☎ 93 318 52 61
🚇 Drassanes, Liceu

MARMALADE
A cocktail bar-cum-
restaurant where an
agreeable mixture of
locals and expats head
for pre-club drinks and
to hob-nob between the
comfy, art deco furniture
and pool table. The
bistro-style food is tasty
and affordable and they
serve an all-day Sunday
brunch.
🟩 F7 ✉ Carrer de Riera
Alta 4–6 ☎ 93 442 39 66
🕐 Mon–Sat evenings only,
Sun all day 🚇 Universitat,
Sant Antoni

MAU MAU
This underground club
in a back street of Poble
Sec is a leading light in
the city's counter culture.
Listen to live music, view
alternative cinema or just
mingle at the bar with
local bohemians. You
may be asked to become
a member, though tour-
ists are generally exempt.
🟩 E8 ✉ Carrer
Fontrodona 33 ☎ 93 441
80 15 🕐 Thu–Sun and for
special events 🚇 Paral·lel

MERCAT DE
LES FLORS
The splendid halls of the
old flower market at the
foot of Montjuïc are now
Barcelona's main venue
for contemporary dance.
As well as being one of
the main scenarios for
the Grec Festival, it also
hosts a number of smaller
festivals and cycles.
🟩 D7 ✉ Carrer de Lleida 59
☎ 93 426 18 75 🚇 Espanya

MOOG
Techno goes full blast
at one of the city's most
popular clubs. Guest DJs
from the international
circuit. Chill-out room.
🟩 F/G8 ✉ Carrer de l'Arc
del Teatre 3 ☎ 93 301 72 82
🕐 Daily 🚇 Drassanes

THE QUIET MAN
One of the city's most
established Irish bars has
live Celtic music Friday
and Saturday.
🟩 G8 ✉ Marqués de
Berbera 11 ☎ 93 412 12 19
🚇 Liceu

SALA APOLO
This hugely popular old
music hall hosts live pop-
rock nightly and dance
clubs Thursday to Sunday.
🟩 G7/8 ✉ Carrer Nou de
la Rambla 113 ☎ 93 441
40 01 🚇 Paral·lel

TABLAO DE CARMEN
This full-blooded flamenco
show in touristy Poble
Espanyol is popular with
locals. You can dine while
watching the show, which
is staged twice nightly.
🟩 C7 ✉ Poble Espanyol
☎ 93 325 68 95 🚇 Espanya
🚌 13, 61

TINTA ROJA
This bar has a bohemian
decor which gives it the
air of an old bordello.
Known for its live tango
music, but occasion-
ally hosts circus acts and
drama groups.
🟩 E7 ✉ Carrer Creu dels
Molers 17 ☎ 93 443 32 43
🚇 Poble Sec

Restaurants

PRICES

Prices are approximate, based on a 3-course meal for one person.

€€€   over €50
€€   €25–€50
€   under €25

ÁNIMA (€€)

This trendy place near the MACBA trumps other eateries in the vicinity by matching the quality of its food to the decor. A preferred place for lunch with local creative types who get there early for the outdoor terrace.

➕ G7 ✉ Carrer de Ángels 6 ☎ 93 342 49 12 🕐 Closed Sun 🚇 Liceu

BASILICO (€)

Buzzing bistro serving light and lovely Mediterranean-meets-Asian dishes such as goat's cheese salad, fresh pastas and fish tempura.

➕ E7 ✉ Avinguda Paral·lel 🚇 Poble Sec 🕐 Daily

CARMELITAS (€)

A great spot for lunch or brunch, which includes wholesome cooking such as roast chicken, goat's cheese salads and burgers, in contemporary yet warm decor.

➕ F7 ✉ Carrer de Doctor Dou 1 ☎ 93 412 46 84 🕐 Daily 🚇 Liceu, San Antoni

LAS FERNANDEZ (€€)

For a taste of something other than Catalan food, head for this outpost of cooking from Leon, where three sisters offer meaty specialties such as dried venison, sausages and hams, as well as light Mediterranean dishes. Bright and cheerful.

➕ F7/8 ✉ Carrer de les Carretes 11 ☎ 93 443 20 43 🕐 Closed Mon and lunch 🚇 Paral·lel

LIA D'EN VICIUS (€)

Wonderfully creative home cooking, either in the cosy, ad-hoc interior or outdoor terrace. A must are the mushroom croquettes, which you could follow with a lentil and mango salad or squid cooked in whisky. Leave room for the rose-petal ice cream.

➕ E8 ✉ Carrer Blai 28 ☎ 93 441 60 72 🕐 Closed 2 weeks in Aug 🚇 Paral·lel

MAM I TECA (€€)

Tiny hole-in-the-wall with few tables and a small bar. Local foodies love the regional tapas that changes most days. Top-notch ingredients.

P AND T

Pa amb tomàquet never fails to comfort a homesick Catalan and no meal is really complete without it. The local version of bread and butter, it consists of a slab of toasted *pa de pagès* (peasant bread) rubbed with a ripe tomato then drizzled with olive oil and spiked with a touch of garlic.

➕ F7 ✉ Carrer de Luna 4 ☎ 93 441 33 35 🕐 Closed Tue and lunch 🚇 Sant Antoni

MESÓN DAVID (€)

This wonderfully lively place offers some of the cheapest food in town. Standards are high and the accent is on Galician cuisine, with *caldo gallego* (cabbage broth) and succulent *lechazo* (roast pork) well to the fore. Sample the almond *tarta de Santiago* for pudding.

➕ F7/8 ✉ Carrer de les Carretes 63 ☎ 93 441 59 34 🕐 Closed Mon 🚇 Paral·lel

QUIMET & QUIMET (€)

More a *bodega* than a bar, this popular joint has a great selection of wine behind the bar and a fantastic selection of tapas.

➕ E8 ✉ Poeta Cabanyes 25 ☎ 93 442 31 42 🕐 Closed Sun, Sat dinner and Aug 🚇 Paral·lel

TICKETS BAR (€€)

Book early for a spot at the city's hottest address: this carnival-themed bar features an exquisite range of gourmet tapas in a relaxed and informal atmosphere. The menu dazzles, with everything from razor clams with lemon 'air' to wafer-thin melt-in-the-mouth ham.

➕ E8 ✉ Avinguda Paral·lel 164 ☎ No phone, reservation by website only, www.ticketsbar.es 🕐 Tue–Fri 7pm–11.30pm, Sat 1.30–3.30, 7–11.30 🚇 Poble Sec

Las Ramblas is Barcelona's magnet, a historic, tree-lined promenade that stretches south from the Plaça de Catalunya to the sea. To its east lies the Barri Gòtic, the ancient city heart.

Las Ramblas and Barri Gòtic

6

7

8

9

Universitat
Central

PLAÇA DE LA
UNIVERSITAT

CARRER DE BALMES

Universitat

RONDA UNIVERSITAT

C DE PELAI

Carrer dels Tallers

Catalunya

Catalunya

RAMBLAS

C santa

Casa Municipal
de Misericòrdia

C. Elisabets

**Las
Ramblas**

C. Pintor Fortuny

Església
de Betlem

Plaça
Vila de
Madrid

CARRER DEL CARME

Palau de la
Virreina

LAS RAMBLAS

**BARRI
GÒTIC**

La Boqueria

**Plaça
de Pí**

CARRER DE L'HOSPITAL

Santa
Maria de Pí

Liceu

**Centre
d'Interpretació
del Call**

Carrer de Sant Pau

C de Boqueria

Gran Teatre
del Liceu

C de Ferran

RAMBLAS

Carrer Nou de la Rambla

**Plaça
Reial**

Palau
Güell

C Nou de St Francesc

C de Codols

C de l'Arc del Teatre

LAS RAMBLAS

Arts Santa
Mònica

**Museu
de Cera**

Drassanes

PLAÇA
DEL PORTAL
DE LA PAU

Carrer J A Clavé

C de

PASSEIG DE

0 ————— 200 m
0 ————— 200 yds

F

G

Plaça
Catalunya

Carrer de   Casp

Urquinaona

PLAÇA
URQUINAONA

Plaça de
Catalunya

Anna

C les Moles

C comtal

VIA LAIETANA

C Magdalenes

Avinguda Portal de l'Àngel

Col·legi
d'Arquitectes

Av Catedral

Museu Diocesà

Museu del
Calçat

Museu
Frederic Marès

Catedral

Plaça del Rei
Museu d'Història
de Barcelona

Palau de la
Generalitat

Plaça de
Sant Jaume

Jaume I

Ajuntament

Carrer Ciutat

VIA LAIETANA

d'Avinyó

Carrer Regomir

C d'En Cignas

Correus
Telègrafs

Església de
la Mercè

Mercè

PLAÇA
D'ANTONI
LÓPEZ

COLOM

H

Las Ramblas and Barri Gòtic

Catedral

HIGHLIGHTS

● Crypt with alabaster tomb of St. Eulàlia
● Late medieval and Renaissance choir stalls
● Capella del Santíssim Sagrament
● Cloister

TIPS

● Remember you will not be able to move around the cathedral during services.
● There are public toilets in the cloister.

This 14th-century cathedral is one of the finest examples of the Catalan Gothic style. It is a noble successor to its Romanesque predecessor and an even older early Christian basilica.

City church Dedicated to an early Christian virgin and martyr, Eulàlia, the cathedral stands firmly in the middle of city life. Weekends see people gather to dance the elegant *sardana*, a stately Catalan folk dance that symbolizes unity. Inside, worshippers easily outnumber tourists. The cloister is a calm refuge from the city with its magnolias, tall palms, fountain and gaggle of geese.

Medley of styles The cathedral was begun at the end of the 13th century and was completed, except for the main facade, by the middle of the

Clockwise from left: the magnificent interior of the Catedral; votive candles at an altar; the imposing Gothic entrance; statues adorning the cathedral exterior; dancers performing the sardana

15th. However, it was not until the mid-19th century that sufficient funds had been accumulated to construct the facade—fashionable but somewhat incongruous in its French-Gothic style. You could spend hours peering at the sometimes faded treasures in the 29 chapels. The most fascinating of these is the old chapter house to the right of the main entrance; beneath a roof rising 20m (65ft) into a star vault is the Christ of Lepanto, a life-size figure carried into the thick of the famous naval battle aboard the royal flagship (▷ 24–25).

The views The elevator on the opposite side of the cloister takes you to the roof from where magnificent panoramic views of the city and the cathedral's spires can be enjoyed from a platform placed over the central nave. The statue perched on top of the highest, central spire is of St. Helen.

THE BASICS

➕ G7
✉ Plaça de la Seu
☎ 93 310 71 95
🕐 Mon–Fri 8–12.45,
5.15–7, Sat 8–12.45, 5.15–6,
Sun during mass only
(cloister 9–12.30, 5.15–6).
Combined Ticket entry
daily 1–5
🚇 Jaume I
🚌 17, 19, 40, 45
♿ Good
💵 Combined Ticket:
moderate (includes elevator and choir, museum);
museum, elevator and
choir: inexpensive; church
and cloister: free

Plaça del Rei

HIGHLIGHTS

Museu d'Història de Barcelona
● Roman city streets, shops and workrooms
● Roman mosaics
● Saló del Tinell
● Chapel of St. Agatha: 15th-century altarpiece by Jaume Huguet

Plaça del Rei
● Steps to the palace
● Linger in an outdoor café

TIP

● Entry to the Museu d' Història de Barcelona gives entry to the Museu Monestir de Pedralbes (▷ 102–103) and a clutch of minor sites.

There is no better way to experience the antiquity of the city than in the Roman settlement of Barcino, the underground world that extends beneath the medieval palace and the Plaça del Rei.

Remains of Roman Barcelona The middle of Roman Barcelona extends beneath Plaça de Sant Jaume and Plaça del Rei, while chunks of its walls protrude elsewhere. One of the best-preserved sections faces Plaça Ramon Berenguer el Gran, next to Plaça del Rei; above the Roman wall and towers are later layers of building, including the medieval Chapel of Santa Agatha.

Museu d'Història de Barcelona (MuHBa) The City History Museum's exhibits trace Barcelona's evolution from Roman trading post to metropolis.

The Casa Padellàs, part of the Museu d'Història de Barcelona (left); the museum was previously a medieval palace (right)

The museum on Plaça del Rei occupies a medieval palace moved here in 1931 when the Via Laietana was driven through the Barri Gòtic. Remains of the old Roman town were revealed by excavations carried out during the rebuilding work. Mosaic floors and parts of surrounding walls are among the underground ruins accessible from the museum. Other relics from Barcelona's history include statues and an oil press.

Regal relics Continue your visit above ground in the medieval palace. The highlight is the arched space of the 14th-century Saló del Tinell, the banquet hall where Columbus was received on his return from the New World. Also visit the exquisite Chapel of Santa Agatha, which contains a remarkable 15th-century gilded altarpiece by Jaume Huguet.

THE BASICS

➕ G8
☎ 93 256 2100
🕐 Tue–Sat 10–7, Sun 10–8. Closed 1 Jan, 1 May, 24 Jun, 24 and 25 Dec
🚇 Jaume I
🚌 17, 19, 40, 45
♿ Poor
🎟 Moderate; free Sun 3–8. Ticket admits to all MuHBa centres around the city, which include the Monestir de Pedralbes (▷ 102–103)
❓ Souvenir and bookshop (entrance Carrer Llibretería); www.museuhistoria.bcn.es

Las Ramblas

HIGHLIGHTS

Starting at Plaça de Catalunya
● Flower market
● Baroque Betlem Church
● 18th-century Palau Moja
● 18th-century Palau de la Virreina information area
● La Boqueria covered market (▷ 48)
● Gran Teatre del Liceu
● Mural by Miró on the pavement at the intersection of Carrer Boqueria
● Arts Santa Mònica
● Museu de Cera (Wax Museum) (▷ 50)

TIPS

● Pickpocketing is rife on the Ramblas, so watch your bag and wallet.
● Bar and restaurant prices are high here and standards low—eat elsewhere.

Supreme among city strolling spaces, the Ramblas stretches from Plaça de Catalunya to the waterfront. Venerable plane trees frame the broad central walkway, which teems with activity.

Pedestrian paradise Most Catalan towns have their Ramblas, a promenade where people go to see and be seen. None, however, enjoys the worldwide fame of Barcelona's. Sooner rather than later, every visitor joins the crowds along this vibrant central space, where strollers rule and traffic is confined to either side. More than a mere thoroughfare, the Ramblas is a place—somewhere to linger, to sit, to rendezvous, to watch street entertainers, to buy a paper, to simply breathe in the essence of the city. Until the 18th century, breathing deeply was highly inadvisable; the

Ramblas owes its origin to an open sewer along the line of the city walls, which once stood here.

More than one Rambla The Ramblas changes its name several times on its way down toward the Columbus Column, just over 1km (half a mile) from Plaça de Catalunya. First comes Rambla de Canaletes with its famous drinking fountain and newsstands, then Rambla dels Estudis, named for the university once sited here. The Rambla de Sant Josep is also known as Rambla de les Flors, after its profusion of flowerstands. The halfway point is marked by Miró's mosaic in the pavement and by Liceu subway station, named after the city's opera house. The Rambla dels Caputxins follows, with its cafés, then the Rambla de Santa Mònica, which has retained its earthy charm despite attempts at modernization.

THE BASICS

✚ G7/8
🚇 Catalunya, Liceu, Drassanes
🚌 14, 59, 91

La Boqueria

TOP 25

La Boqueria is famous for its excellent selection of fresh fish, fruit and vegetables

THE BASICS

www.boqueria.infot
- G7
- 93 412 13 15
- Closed on Sun. Fish section closed on Mon
- Liceu
- 14, 59, 91
- Good

HIGHLIGHTS

- Breakfast or lunch at one of the traditional counter bars
- Superb selection of fresh fish
- Exotic goodies from around the world

TIP

- The stalls nearest the front tend to have tourist prices – head to the back for more reasonable prices.

Barcelona's central market is a much-loved city landmark. Although the official name is Mercat de Sant Josep, it's better known as La Boqueria. It's a fabulous place to eat, pick up exotic picnic goodies or simply soak up the atmosphere.

Medieval beginnings The market dates back to the 12th century, but it wasn't until the 19th century that it was covered. The elegant *modernista* sign, made of jewel-coloured stained glass, was added in 1912, and the market has been expanded twice since. It is Barcelona's largest and best-known market, famous for its incredible range of produce, which features not only the best Catalan meat, fish, fruit and vegetables, but also goods from around the world.

Stands At the front of the market, nearest the main entrance, you'll find many of the crowd-pleasing fruit and juice stalls, but it's worth plunging deeper to discover some of the most enticing stands. Don't miss the fabulous fish section (closed Mondays), where you can gawp at an eye-popping range of marine life laid out on piles of shaved ice.

Eating and drinking The market is not just a great place to ogle piles of gleaming seafood, fruits and vegetables and meat, it's also full of wonderful counter bars where you can tuck into a range of cuisines. Most serve traditional Catalan dishes, but you'll also find sushi, veggie options, fresh juices and more.

Shopping in the Barri Gòtic

Fans for sale (left) in one of the Barri Gòtic's many specialist shops (right)

Barcelona's Barri Gòtic, the oldest part of the city, is a dense maze of shops, cafés, alleyways and squares. You'll find antiques dealers, galleries and gourmet food stores side by side with quirky boutiques and fast-food outlets.

North of the Plaça del Pí Start at the corner of the Ramblas and the Carrer de la Portaferrissa. Portaferrissa is one of the *barri's* busiest shopping streets, with a wide selection of cheap and cheerful fashion stores aimed squarely at the young. Walk down and take the second right onto Carrer de Petritxol where clothes shops give way to chic galleries selling antiques and pictures, including landscapes and city scenes of Catalonia and Barcelona. At the end of Petritxol you'll find yourself in picturesque Plaça del Pí. The adjoining Plaça de Sant Josep Oriol has an art market every Saturday and some good home decor shops. Several good shopping streets branch off the square. Take Carrer de la Palla to track down food specialties and some wonderfully old-fashioned toy stores.

South of the Plaça del Pí Alternatively, take Carrer de l'Ave Maria out of Oriol and turn left onto the top section of Carrer dels Banys Nous. Here you'll find boutiques concentrating on beads and dress jewellery, lovely bags and craft and designer goods. Heading south; there's a splendid old-fashioned hat shop at the junction with Carrer de la Palla and more trinket, jewellery and shoe and ethnic clothing shops along the Carrer Boqueria.

THE BASICS

+ G7–G8
🚇 Liceu, Catalunya
🚌 14, 38, 59, 91

HIGHLIGHTS

● Browsing at the weekend markets
● An outside table at the Bar del Pi on the Plaça del Pí is the perfect place for people-watching
● Recharge your energy with a sugar fix at any of the *granjas* (cake and coffee shops) along the Carrer Petrixol. Try a *suizo*: a thick hot chocolate topped with whipped cream

More to See

CENTRE D'INTERPRETACIÓ DEL CALL

This information and exhibition centre aims to explain the history and culture of El Call, Barcelona's medieval Jewish community that once thrived deep in the Barri Gòtic. They can advise you on where to see its remaining vestiges, including an ancient synagogue.

🕂 G8 ☒ Placeta de Manuel Ribe s/n ☎ 93 256 21 00 🕐 Wed–Fri 10–2, Sat 11–6, Sun 11–3 🚇 Liceu

MUSEU DE CERA

www.museocerabcn.com

Housed in a lovely 19th-century stately building, the wax museum in the Rambla is charmingly old-fashioned, though a real kids-pleaser.

🕂 G8 ☒ Passatge de la Banca 7 ☎ 93 317 26 49 🕐 Mid-Jul to 24 Sep daily 10–10.30; 25 Sep to mid-Jul Mon–Fri 10–2, 4–8, Sun 11–2, 4.30–8.30 💷 Expensive 🚇 Drassanes

MUSEU FREDERIC MARÈS

www.museumares.bcn.cat

There are three main reasons for visiting this museum named after the sculptor and obsessive collector Frederic Marès: its setting overlooking the courtyard garden of the Royal Palace; its collection of sculpture from pre-Roman times to the 19th century; and the section known as the Collecìò Sentimental, with its surreal array of everyday objects from the 15th to the 19th centuries. Marès' studio and library have been preserved on the top floors.

🕂 G7 ☒ Plaça Sant lu 5 ☎ 93 310 58 00 🕐 Tue–Sat 10–7, Sun 10–8 🍴 Café 🚇 Jaume I ♿ Few ✋ Moderate. Free 1st Sun of month and Wed and Sun from 3pm

PLAÇA DE CATALUNYA

City life seems to revolve around this spacious central square, not least because of its position at the upper end of the Ramblas. The main landmark is the huge slablike Corte Inglès department store; it is also the location of the largest tourist office and the principal transport stop-off. You can catch a bus or train connection to anywhere in town, including the airport. The number of monuments

An exhibit at the Museu de Cera

Detail of a mother and child statue in the Museu Frederic Marès

and statues is considerable and well worth a look. A 1991 addition commemorates the popular pre-Civil War politician Francesc Macià.

🚹 G7 🚇 Catalunya

PLAÇA DEL PÍ

Set amid the warren of winding streets between the cathedral and the Ramblas you'll find Plaça del Pí and the adjoining Plaça Sant Josep, two of Barcelona's most beguiling squares. These asymmetrical spaces have leafy shade, laid-back cafés and weekend art exhibitions. A great place to relax, Pí is named for the pine trees that once grew here, as is the serene church, Santa Maria del Pí. The monumentally plain exterior of this Barri Gòtic church conceals an equally austere interior—a single nave in characteristic Catalan Gothic style. The main facade, its statues long since gone, has a fine rose window. The octagonal bell tower is 55m (180ft) high.

🚹 G7/8 🕐 Church: daily 9.30–12.30, 5–8 🚇 Liceu

PLAÇA REIAL

With its arcades and classical facades, this grandiose and splendidly symmetrical square is in complete contrast to the crooked streets and alleyways of the surrounding Barri Gòtic. Built in the mid-19th century on the model of the squares of Paris, it is a preferred hangout of idlers and winos, though it is considerably smarter than it once was. Antoni Gaudí designed the sinuous, wrought-iron lampposts, his first official commission by the city of Barcelona in the 1870s.

🚹 G8 🚇 Liceu

PLAÇA DE SANT JAUME

The Plaça de Sant Jaume has been the administrative heart of the city since Roman times, when the square was occupied by the Forum. It remains home to the city's most important public institutions: the Ajuntament (City Hall) and the Palau de la Generalit (home to the Catalan regional government).

🚹 G8 🚇 Liceu, Jaume I 🚌 14, 17, 19, 38, 40, 45, 59, 91

The arcaded oasis of the Plaça Reial

The Barri Gòtic

A stroll round the heart of the Barri Gòtic that takes you past some of its main sights.

DISTANCE: 1.5km (1 mile) **ALLOW:** 45–60 minutes

START

PLAÇA DE L'ÀNGEL
🚇 G8 🚇 Jaume I

1 With your back to the large thoroughfare, Via Laietana, look for the road to your right, Baixada de la Llibreteria. Walk along to the intersection with Carrer de Veguer. Turn right.

2 Walk to the end to the Plaça del Rei. With your back to the *plaça*, take the right-hand exit onto Baixada de Santa Clara. You then come to the rear of the cathedral (▷ 42).

3 Turn right along Carrer dels Comtes (the cathedral is on your left). Continue ahead, pass the Museu Frederic Marès (▷ 50) and continue onto the Plaça de la Seu.

4 Take an immediate left onto Carrer de Santa Llùcia. Turn left onto Carrer de Bisbe and then turn hard right onto the winding Montjuïc del Bisbe to the square of Sant Felip Neri.

END

PLAÇA DE L'ÀNGEL
🚇 Jaume I

8 Turn right where the road name changes to Carrer de la Dagueria. At the intersection with Carrer de la Jaume I, turn right. The Plaça de l'Àngel, where you started, is on the left. The metro station, Jaume I, is also here.

7 Continue down Carrer del Regomir then turn left onto Carrer del Correu Vell. In a few steps the street becomes Carrer de Lledó. Continue ahead past Plaça de Sant Just.

6 Turn left onto Carrer del Call and continue to the immense Plaça de Sant Jaume (▷ 51). Bear right and take Carrer de la Ciutat, which eventually becomes Carrer del Regomir.

5 Take the farthest exit out of the square onto Carrer de Sant Felip Neri. Turn left onto Carrer de Sant Domenech del Call.

Shopping

ALAMACENES DE PILAR

For combs, shawls, fans, feathers and all Spanish finery, this large shop has the best selection. Items include spotted flamenco dresses and bolts of silk brocade. Prices range from a few euros for a wooden fan, to hundreds for a richly embroidered silk *mantilla* (shawl).
🔳 G8 ✉ Carrer Boqueria 43 ☎ 93 317 79 84 Ⓜ Liceu

ART ESCUDELLERS

If it's local ceramics or glassware you are after, this is the place. Wares are laid out by region, from the simple terra-cotta and green pottery of Catalonia to more intricate, hand-painted tiles and other ceramics from Valencia and Andalucia. One-off pieces from local artists are also available. Despite its touristy look, prices are reasonable.
🔳 G8 ✉ Carrer Escudellers 23 ☎ 93 412 68 01 Ⓜ Drassanes

BARRI GÒTIC ANTIQUES MARKET

Bric-à-brac rather than heirloom bargains dominate the stands in front of the cathedral. From 20 November to 21 December the market moves to the adjacent Portal de l'Angel and a Christmas market takes its place.
🔳 G7 ✉ Avinguda de la Catedral 6 🕐 Thu 9–8 Ⓜ Jaume I

CAELUM

All over Spain nuns in their convents produce delicious cakes, biscuits and sweets, make candles, scented soap and exquisite embroidery. Caelum stocks such delights, beautifully packaged, and there's a café to sample before you buy.
🔳 G7 ✉ Carrer de la Palla 8 ☎ 93 302 69 93 Ⓜ Liceu, Jaume I

CERERIA SUBIRÁ

Dating from 1761, this is supposedly the oldest shop in the city. Started as a ladies' outfitters, it now sells candles in all shapes and sizes. Staff with starched uniforms seem to come from another era.
🔳 G8 ✉ Baixada de Llibreteria 7 ☎ 93 315 26 06 Ⓜ Jaume I

EL CORTE INGLÉS

Virtually everything you could ever need under the roof of an aircraft-carrier-like establishment. On the several floors between the supermarket in the basement and the restaurant-café at the top are designer fashions, cosmetics, jewels, computers and more. A satellite branch at Portal de l'Angel sells sports clothing/equipment and music.
🔳 G7 ✉ Plaça de Catalunya 14 ☎ 901 122 122 Ⓜ Catalunya

COSES DE CASA

This fabulous, wood-panelled shop in Plaça Sant Josep Orol specializes in unusual upholstery fabrics, featuring ethnic-inspired prints, weaves and embroidery. Some are made up into take-home goodies such as toiletry bags, cushion covers and gorgeous throws.
🔳 G7 ✉ Plaça Sant Josep Oriol 5 ☎ 93 302 73 28 Ⓜ Liceu

DA VINCI COLORS

Manoletes, or ballet pumps, are the only style of shoe stocked here, but they come in a myriad of leathers, suedes and colours. 'Surprise' stocks arrive on Fridays (even the sales assistants are unsure of the content).
🔳 G8 ✉ Carrer Boqueria 30 Ⓜ Liceu

FORMATGERIA LA SEU

This shop is dedicated to Spanish and Catalan cheeses. Pop in for a

WHAT TO BUY IN THE BARRI GÒTIC

The intricate streets and alleyways of the old town east of the Rambla are full of individual shops selling virtually everything you might want to either eat or admire. There are craftspeople's candles, cured hams and all kinds of antiques and art objects. Portaferrissa and Portal de l'Angel streets have fashion boutiques and shoe shops.

tasting with wine, before stocking up on hard-to-get treats to take home.
🟥 G8 ✉ Carrer de la Dagueria 16 ☎ 93 412 65 48 🚇 Jaume 1

GANIVETERÍA
If you're looking for the perfect knife, shears, scissors, penknife or blade of any type, this long-established store has one of the largest ranges in Europe; it also offers a sharpening service.
🟥 G7 ✉ Plaça del Pí 3 ☎ 93 302 12 41 🚇 Liceu, Jaume I

HERBORISTERÍA DEL REI
Since 1860 this well-loved shop has been selling all types of dried herbs, infusions and natural cures. In keeping with the times, organic olive oils and cosmetics are a new addition.
🟥 G8 ✉ Carrer del Vidre 1 ☎ 93 318 05 12 🚇 Liceu

EL INGENIO
Even if you are not in the market for a carnival costume, this shop will delight. El Ingenio is like stepping into a giant dress-up box, with a cornucopia of costumes, masks, wigs and party tricks and novelties. At the back there are some *capgrosses* on display (papier mâché heads that are marched out during the city's celebrations).
🟥 G8 ✉ Carrer Rauric 6 ☎ 93 317 71 38 🚇 Liceu

JOGUINES MONFORTE
This superbly traditional shop specializes in old-fashioned board games for adults and kids, as well as jigsaw puzzles, wooden solitaire boards and chess sets. Snap up a game of *parchís* (ludo) or *el juego del oca* (the goose game), a Spanish-style snakes and ladders.
🟥 G7 ✉ Plaça Sant Josep Oriol 3 ☎ 93 318 22 85 🚇 Liceu

LA MANUAL ALPARGATERA
All kinds of rope-soled shoes, some created before your eyes. The specialty is *espadenyas*, or espadrilles.
🟥 G8 ✉ Carrer d'Avinyó 7 ☎ 93 301 01 72 🚇 Liceu

MOSTRA D'ART
This art market takes place in one of the Barri Gòtic's most picturesque squares. Worth a browse.
🟥 G7 ✉ Plaça Sant Josep Oriol 🕐 Sat 11–8.30, Sun 11–2.30 🚇 Liceu

PICNIC PLACES
Look out for the offerings from the *forn de pa* (bakery) and the *xarcuteria* (delicatessen or charcuterie). Don't miss slicings from a good *jamón serrano* (dry-cured ham). Look for *fuet* (a hard Catalan sausage), *chorizo*, *sabrasada* (a Mallorcan paste of pork and paprika), and cured *Manchego* cheese.

PAPABUBBLE
Kids will adore this concept candy shop, where the goodies are made on the spot, so you can watch them roll, twist and form the soft candy into unusual shapes, and have them personalize it for you. The tastes are as unique as the packaging; ask to try the flower and cocktail combinations.
🟥 G8 ✉ Carrer Ample 28 ☎ 93 268 86 25 🚇 Jaume I

SALA PARÉS
The city's best art gallery, showing works of leading Catalan artists.
🟥 G8 ✉ Petritxol 5 ☎ 93 318 70 20 🚇 Liceu

EL TRIANGLE
This complex contains, among other shops, FNAC and Habitat. FNAC is one of the city's best sources for books, with a large English section, videos and CDs and a ticket office for visiting musical concerts. The perfume and cosmetics shop, Sephora, is also here.
🟥 G7 ✉ Plaça de Catalunya 4 ☎ 93 318 01 08 🚇 Catalunya

VAHO GALLERY
Banner bags, or bags and luggage made out of recycled PVC banners, are all the rage in Barcelona. Vaho were the pioneers and their items make unique souvenirs.
🟥 G7 ✉ Plaça Sant Josep Oriol 3 ☎ 93 412 78 94 🚇 Liceu

Entertainment and Nightlife

BARCELONA PIPA CLUB

Its days as a famous jazz club have long gone (although they still regularly host free gigs featuring a range of musical styles) but the Pipa club lives on as a popular watering hole for nighthawks. Ring the street-level bell to gain entrance.

➕ G8 ✉ Plaça Reial 3, pral ☎ 93 302 47 32 🚇 Liceu, Drassanes

GRAN TEATRE DEL LICEU

Destroyed by fire in 1861, rebuilt, then burned again in 1994, the Lyceum holds a special place in the hearts of musical Barcelonins, since it was here that the city's passion for opera found its prime expression. The building can be toured at 10am daily or inspected without a guide at 11.30, noon, 12.30 and 1.

➕ G8 ✉ Rambla 61–65 ☎ 93 485 99 00 (93 485 99 14 to arrange visits) 🚇 Liceu

HARLEM JAZZ CLUB

Barcelona's oldest jazz club has certainly moved with the times and still packs in the crowds who come to enjoy some of the most varied music in the city—everything from jazz to flamenco fusion.

➕ G8 ✉ Carrer de la Comtessa de Sobradiel 8 ☎ 93 310 07 55 🕐 Closed Sun, 2 weeks in Aug 🚇 Jaume I

JAMBOREE

An underground jazz club that's almost cavelike, hosting blues, soul, jazz, funk and occasional hip-hop live bands. At 1am on weekends, the dance floor opens and gets crowded quite quickly.

➕ G8 ✉ Plaça Reial 17 ☎ 93 319 17 89 🕐 Daily 9pm–5am 🚇 Liceu

JAMSONIK

If it's budget drinks and a young, raucous up-for-it crowd you are after, here's the place. Most people seem to be on a holiday, or oblivious to hangovers.

➕ G7 ✉ Las Ramblas 116 🚇 Liceu

KARMA

This basement venue is still the most popular of several lively rock clubs around Plaça Reial.

➕ G9 ✉ Plaça Reial 10 ☎ 93 302 56 80 🕐 Tue–Sun midnight–5am 🚇 Liceu

NIGHT ZONES

Vigorous nightlife takes place all over the city. Plaça Reial in the old town is always active, though new laws on noise levels have pushed many late-night clubs out of the inner city and into the suburbs, where the action takes place until dawn and beyond. The Eixample area has plenty of classy cocktail bars and summer terraces while Gràcia and Poble Sec offer a more low-key vibe.

LA MACARENA

This tiny techno club in the back streets of the Barri Gòtic pulls in plenty of punters post 2am. International DJs regularly play here, and the miniscule dance floor gets jam packed. Expect to queue.

➕ G8 ✉ Carrer Nou de Sant Francesc 5 🕐 Mon–Thu, Sun 11.30–4.30, Fri–Sat 11.30–5.30 🚇 Drassanes

MENAGE À TROIS

As the name suggests, this intimate little bar is more apt for a quiet cocktail and bar food, either inside or out overlooking the Roman remains in Plaça Vila de Madrid.

➕ G7 ✉ Carrer d' en Bot 4 ☎ 93 301 55 42 🕐 Closed Mon 🚇 Catalunya

SMOLL

A pop feel dominates here, with original objects from the 50s to 70s dotted around (which are for sale). Cocktails are the thing to order, the perfect drink for the bar's lounge music soundtrack.

➕ G8 ✉ Carrer de la Comtessa de Sobradiel 9 ☎ 686 303 095 🕐 Closed Sun 🚇 Jaume I

LOS TARANTOS

Here you will find some of the best flamenco acts in Catalonia. Conveniently located in Plaça Reial. Most gigs start at 8.30pm, and there are several in one evening.

➕ G8 ✉ Plaça Reial 17 ☎ 93 319 17 89 🚇 Liceu

Restaurants

PRICES

Prices are approximate, based on a 3-course meal for one person.
€€€   over €50
€€   €25–€50
€   under €25

AGUT (€€)

The Agut family, which has owned the restaurant for the last three generations, has a menu reflecting seasonal availability as well as dishes that are popular all year round, such as *olla barrejada* (a Catalan stew with vegetables and meat) and *fideuà* (fish noodles), cod with red peppers and garlic mayonnaise.
✚ G8 ✉ Carrer d'en Gignàs 16 ☎ 93 315 17 09 🕐 Tue–Sat 1.30–4, 9–12, Sun 1–4; closed Aug 🚇 Jaume I

BAR DEL PÍ (€)

Friendly service at this tapas bar delightfully located in the little square dominated by the church of Santa Maria del Pí.
✚ G7 ✉ Plaça Sant Josep Oriol 🕐 Closed Mon 🚇 Liceu

LA BODEGA DE PALMA (€)

This rustic, old-school tapas bar is equally as popular with locals as visitors. Get here around 8.30pm to grab one of the tiny marble tables and order marinated sardines and homemade omelette or share a plate of stuffed peppers over a jug of barrel wine. Service is tourist-friendly without being touristy.
✚ G8 ✉ Carrer Palma de Sant Just 7 ☎ 93 315 06 56 🕐 Mon–Fri 9am–midnight, Sat noon–midnight 🚇 Jaume I

BOSCO (€)

This charming restaurant behind the cathedral, serves tapas (including their delectable *patatas Bosco*—a variation of the classic *patatas bravas*), as well as more substantial meals. Fresh, modern Mediterranean dishes might include oven-baked turbot, or canelones with wild mushrooms. There's a great-value set lunch menu.
✚ G8 ✉ Carrer Capellans 9 ☎ 93 412 13 70 🕐 Mon 1–5, Tue–Sat 1–3.30, 8–11.30 🚇 Liceu, Jaume I

CAFÉ DE L'ACADEMIA (€€)

Not really a café at all, this restaurant offers some of the best deals

in town on a variety of traditional Mediterranean cuisine. Reserve ahead.
✚ G8 ✉ Carrer de Lledó 1 ☎ 93 319 82 53 🕐 Closed weekends, 3 weeks in Aug 🚇 Jaume I

CAFÉ DE L'OPERA (€)

Opera goers and tourists fill the art nouveau interior and terrace tables of this dignified establishment opposite the Liceu. A great place for a spot of people-watching on the Rambla, but the coffees, drinks and snacks don't come cheap.
✚ G8 ✉ Rambla 74 ☎ 93 317 75 85 🕐 Daily 🚇 Liceu

CAN CULLERETES (€€)

Can Culleretes has the distinction of being one of the oldest restaurants in the city, founded in 1786 as a pastry shop. The menu is like a catalogue of old-fashioned Catalan cuisine, but there are modern dishes, too. Sample the *botifarra* (pork sausage) with white beans.
✚ G8 ✉ Carrer d'en Quintana 5 ☎ 93 317 30 22 🕐 Closed Sun evening, Mon, Jul 🚇 Liceu

LA CUINA DEL DO (€€€)

Part of one of the city's newest five-star hotels, this elegant restaurant in a stone-vaulted dining room is renowned for its contemporary Catalan cuisine. Choose between the set menus or go à la

carte, and enjoy dishes such as lamb terrine with asparagus and artichokes, or tomato salad with smoked sardines.

🔶 G8 ⊠ Plaça Reial 1 ☎ 93 481 36 66 🕓 Tue–Sat 1.30–3.30, 7.30–11 🚇 Liceu

JUICY JONES (€)

A hot spot for vegetarians, this juice bar churns out every combination of juices and smoothies, as well as filled baguettes, Indian rice, couscous dishes and great salads—and it's all fresh and vegan-friendly.

🔶 G8 ⊠ Carrer del Cardenal Casañas 7 ☎ 93 302 43 30 🕓 Daily 🚇 Liceu

KOY SHUNKA (€€€)

This is considered one of the best Japanese restaurants in the city, as its clientele of star chefs and local gastronomes confirms. You'll need to reserve, though there are often seats left at the bar where you'll be entertained by the masterful sushi chefs.

🔶 G8 ⊠ Carrer Copons 7 ☎ 93 412 79 39 🕓 Closed Mon and 2 weeks in Aug 🚇 Jaume I

PEIMONG (€)

Peimong draws a crowd for its tasty Peruvian cuisine. Its *ceviche* (fish marinated in lime juice) really zings and more hearty dishes include *lomo saltado* (pork with onions and tomatoes), best washed down with an 'Inca' brand cola or beer.

🔶 G8 ⊠ Carrer Templars 6 ☎ 93 318 28 73 🕓 Closed Sun dinner, Mon 🚇 Jaume I

PLA (€€)

An excellent spot for a romantic meal in the Barri Gòtic. The chef draws on the influences of Mediterranean, vegetarian and international cooking. There's a wide selection of carpaccio: fish with prawns, duck *magret*, sometimes a couscous. The crêpes with nuts and the sautéed vegetables with chicken are good, but a house special is the tuna *tataki* with lime leaves in a citrus and coconut sauce.

🔶 G8 ⊠ Carrer de Bellafila 5 ☎ 93 412 65 52 🕓 Dinner only daily 🚇 Jaume I

CATALAN COOKING

Catalonia is generally reckoned to have one of the great regional cuisines of Spain. It is based on good ingredients from the varied countryside and on seafood from the Mediterranean and the Atlantic. Four principal sauces are used. There is *sofregit* (onion, tomato and garlic cooked in olive oil); with added sweet pepper, aubergine and courgette it becomes *samfaina*. *Picada* is made by pounding nuts, fried bread, parsley, saffron and other ingredients in a mortar. Finally there is garlic mayonnaise, *alioli*.

ELS QUATRE GATS (€€)

The Four Cats was frequented by Barcelona's 20th-century bohemian crowd (including Picasso), two of whom are depicted in the famous picture (a reproduction) of arty types riding a tandem bicycle. There is a tapas bar up front, while the restaurant is situated in the back.

🔶 G7 ⊠ Montsió 3bis ☎ 93 302 41 40 🕓 Daily 🚇 Urquinaona, Catalunya

TALLER DE TAPAS (€)

Unashamedly aimed at tourists wanting to try tapas but wary of ordering across the counter, this congenial tapas bar has multilingual menus and plenty of seating—the tapas are excellent, particularly the seafood and vegetable dishes.

🔶 G7 ⊠ Plaça Sant Josep Oriol 9 ☎ 93 301 80 20 🕓 Daily 🚇 Liceu

VINATERIA DEL CALL (€)

This low-ceilinged, Gothic-looking bodega is perceived to be one of the best places to taste *pa amb tomaquèt*, the ubiquitous Catalan 'tomato bread' (▷ 38). Try it with all sorts of cheese and charcuterie, accompanied by a glass of rioja from their excellent wine list.

🔶 G8 ⊠ Carrer Sant Domenec del Call 9 ☎ 93 302 60 92 🕓 Dinner only daily 🚇 Liceu

Port Vell has been transformed from a rundown industrial dock area into a waterside pleasure zone. Inland lies the historic Ribera, whose two sections, Sant Pere and the Born, are rich in urban pleasures.

5

6

7

8

9

Carrer de Girona Casp

CARRER DE BAILÈN

PASSEIG DE SANT JOAN

Casa Calvet

Carrer del Bruc

d'Ausiàs

RONDA DE SANT PERE

CARRER

Carrer

Arc de Triomf

DE TRAFALGAR

Palau de la Música Catalana

Arc del Triomf

Plaça St Pere

CASC ANTIC

Carrer Sant Pere Mitjà

C Cortines

Carrer Sant Pere més Baix

C Portal Nou

PASSEIG

Av F Cambó

Giralt

Merges

Cargers

LLUÍS COMPANYS

Mercat Santa Caterina

C del Comerç

PICASSO

Museu de Ciències Naturals

Museu de Xocolata

CARRER DE LA PRINCESA

Museu de Geologia

DHUB Montcada

Museu Picasso

PASSEIG

Carrer de comercial

Museu Barbier-Mueller d'Art Precolombí

Passeig del Born

Montcada

Mercat del Born

DE

Santa Maria del Mar

RIBERA

VIA LAIETANA

C. Consolat de Mar

Plaça del Palau

AVINGUDA MARQUÈS DE L'ARGENTERA

La Llotja

PLAÇA D'ANTONI PG ISABEL II LÓPEZ

ESTACIÓ BARCELONA DE FRANÇA

PASSEIG

DE

250 m

250 yds

Moll de Bosch i Alsina

Barceloneta

CARRER DEL DR AIGUADER

Palau de Mar

Plaça de Pau Vila

RONDA

Dàrsena Nacional

Moll d'Espanya

Museu d'Història de Catalunya

CARRER DEL DR AIGUADER

LITORAL

Carrer de Balboa

PASSEIG DE JOAN DE BORBÓ

Reial Club Marítim

Dàrsena del Comerç

Plaça de Pompeu Fabrà

Parc de la Barceloneta

Port Vell

L'Aquàrium

Moll de la Barceloneta

Plaça Barceloneta

Plaça de la Font

BARCELONETA

C d'Andrea Dòria

Poliesportiu Marítim

Carrer sant Carles

Plaça Brugada

San Miquel del Port

Carrer Almirall Cervera

Passeig

Platja

G

H

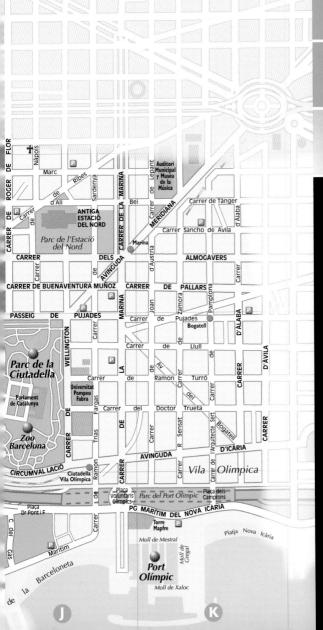

Barceloneta

TOP 25

The popular beach at Barceloneta (left); a fish sculpture (right)

THE BASICS

➕ H/J9

✉ Barceloneta

🚇 Barceloneta

🚌 17, 39, 45, 57, 64, 157

❓ Barceloneta's Festa Major, with music, parades, dancing on the beach and fireworks runs through the 3rd week in Sep

HIGHLIGHTS

● Plaça Barceloneta with baroque church of San Miquel del Port
● The Mercat de Barceloneta
● Market on Plaça de la Font
● Passeig Marítim
● The beaches

The cramped streets of Barceloneta evoke the culture of a traditional Mediterranean fishing village. Cut off from the rest of the city for years, this vibrant area has its own atmosphere and identity.

Little Barcelona Displaced by the building of the Ciutadella (▷ 66), many people from the Ribera moved to live in shanty dwellings between the port and the sea. In 1751 the shacks were swept away, the land reclaimed and this new triangular district, Barceloneta, was developed. Designed by French army engineer, Prosper Verboom, it comprises long narrow blocks of identical housing, the regularity broken by squares. By the 19th century the *barri* had become the home of dock workers and fishermen, divided from the rest of the city by the construction of a rail-and-road barrier at one end.

Moves of change During the 1990s, the whole of the Port Vell (▷ 68–69) was redeveloped, and the northern end of Passeig Joan de Borbó became a smart waterfront promenade and marina. The famous *chiringuitos*, basic seafood restaurants that once lined the waterfront, were swept away, the beach added and its surroundings landscaped. Barceloneta itself has undergone a transformation, with a new market, more housing and Benedetta Tagliabue's glittering glass-faced Natural Gas building. The *barri's* symbol has become Estel Ferit *(Wounded Star)*, a sculpture of three stacked cubes on the beach, though this may soon be swapped for the new sail-shaped W Hotel on the beach, a sign of the *barri's* further gentrification.

Museu Picasso

The exterior of the museum (left and middle); a painting from Las Meninas *(right)*

Picasso, the greatest painter of modern times, came to live in Barcelona at the age of 14. Many of his formative experiences took place in the old town and a museum devoted to his work is here.

Picasso's palace The Picasso Museum's collection concentrates on certain periods of Picasso's life and artistic evolution, including his time in Barcelona. The work benefits enormously from its setting; the magnificent Palau Berenguer d'Aguilar and four adjacent buildings give an excellent idea of the lifestyle enjoyed by the merchant families at the height of medieval Barcelona's prosperity.

At home and away An Andalucian hailing from Malaga, Pablo Ruiz Picasso accompanied his art teacher father and family to Barcelona in 1895. His skills flourished at his father's academy and later, at art school in Madrid. Beginning in 1899, he immersed himself in bohemian Barcelona, frequenting the red-light district centred on Carrer d'Avinyó, the inspiration for *Demoiselles d'Avignon* (1907). He became an habitué of Els Quatre Gats (Four Cats, ▷ 58), a café whose menu he designed. His first exhibition was held here in 1900, the year he made his first visit to Paris. France was to be his real home after that, but he returned to Barcelona many times, and much of the work in his Blue Period (c. 1902–04) was carried out here. The Civil War, which provoked one of his most passionate paintings, *Guernica*—now in the Centro Nacional de Arte Reina Sofía in Madrid—put an end to these visits.

THE BASICS

www.museupicasso.bcn.es

➕ H8

✉ Carrer Montcada 15–23

☎ 93 256 30 00

🕐 Tue–Sun 10–8. Closed 1 Jan, 1 May, 24 Jun, 25–26 Dec

🍴 Café-restaurant

Ⓜ Jaume I

🚌 17, 19, 40, 45

♿ Good

💰 Moderate; free Sun after 3pm

HIGHLIGHTS

- Ceramics from 1940s and 1950s
- *The Embrace* (1900)
- *Science and Charity* (1897)
- *Gored Horse* (1917)
- *El Loco* (The Madman) (1904)
- *Harlequin* (1917)
- *Las Meninas* suite (1957)
- Cannes paintings of landscapes and doves (late 1950s)

Palau de la Música Catalana

TOP 25

The elaborate exterior of the concert hall (left) and the interior (right)

THE BASICS

www.palaumusica.org
🔢 H7
✉ Carrer Palau de la Música 4–6
☎ 93 295 72 00
🕐 Guided visits daily 10–3.30; Jul, Aug and Easter Week daily 10–6
🍴 Bar
🚇 Urquinaona
🚌 17, 19, 40, 45
♿ Good
💶 Expensive (tickets from ticket office in advance)

HIGHLIGHTS

Main facade
● Catalan songsters in mosaic
● Composers' busts
● Proscenium sculpture *Allegory of Catalan Folksong*
● Foyer vaults with floral capitals
● Bust of Pau (Pablo) Casals (given 1936)
● Stained glass inverted dome in the concert hall

For nearly a century, this glittering jewel has served not only as a concert hall but also as an icon of Catalan cultural life. The profusion of ornament is staggering—a delight in itself.

Catalan icon The sumptuous Palace of Catalan Music was designed by the great *modernista* architect Domènech i Montaner as the home of the Catalan national choir, the Orfeó. It was inaugurated in 1908 to unanimous acclaim and became a symbol of the new renaissance in Catalan culture. Montaner gave the building a steel frame to support profuse interior and exterior decoration intended to inspire and instruct. This decoration was the work of his own ceramicists, painters, glassworkers and tilers.

Art-full auditorium Riches encrust the main facade, the entrance hall, the foyer and staircase, but the 2,000-seat concert hall is even more ornate. Light pours in through the transparent walls and from the roof, from which hangs an extraordinary bowl of stained glass. The proscenium arch, far from being a static frame, seems to swell and move, such is the dynamism of its pale pumice sculptures. On the left, a willow tree shelters the great mid-19th-century reviver of Catalan music, Josep Anselm Clavé; on the right a bust of Beethoven is upstaged by Wagnerian Valkyries rollicking through the clouds. Equally stunning is the curving wall at the back of the stage, from which emerge the 18 Muses of music. Reserve in advance for a performance.

Palau de Mar

Dispel any ignorance of Catalonia's past with a visit to the entertaining Palau de Mar, home to the Museu d'Història de Catalunya. Innovative and interactive exhibits clarify what has gone into the creation of this nation within a nation.

Catalonia! Catalonia! An imposing late 19th-century warehouse houses this stimulating museum. Although Catalan history may be something of a mystery to casual visitors, it's worth knowing more about—the past speaks volumes about the present and current aspirations. General Franco wanted Catalan identity to disappear altogether; the museum is one of many initiatives that the regional government (the Generalitat) took to restore it. The exhibits have detailed Catalan explanations and simple English ones, and you can get an English guide at the ticket desk.

Intriguing exhibits The waterfront museum highlights themes from history in a series of spaces grouped around a central atrium. There are few objects on display, but exhibits are truly ingenious; you can work an Arab waterwheel, walk over a skeleton in its shallow grave, climb on to a cavalier's charger and test the weight of his armour, enter a medieval forest, peer into a primitive stone cabin, enjoy a driver's-eye view from an early tram, and cower in a Civil War air-raid shelter. Sound effects, films and interactive screens enhance the experience and the temporary shows, which deal with aspects of Catalonia's history, are of a very high standard.

THE BASICS

www.mhcat.net
+ H9
✉ Plaça de Pau Vila 3
☎ 93 225 47 00
🕐 Tue, Thu–Sat 10–7, Wed 10–8, Sun 10–2.30
🍴 Café
Ⓜ Barceloneta
🚌 14, 17, 39, 57, 59, 64
♿ Good
💶 Moderate

HIGHLIGHTS

● Early ship packed with amphorae
● Moorish market stall
● Sinister Civil Guards pursuing insurgents
● Civil War machine-gun emplacement
● Franco-era schoolroom
● 1930s kitchen with objects to handle
● First edition of George Orwell's *Homage to Catalonia*
● 1960s tourist bar with *Speak Inglis/Parle Frances* sign

Parc de la Ciutadella

Steps leading to the park (left); the Arc de Triomf (right)

THE BASICS

✚ H/J8

🚇 Arc de Triomf, Barceloneta

🚌 14, 39, 41, 59

HIGHLIGHTS

● The Cascada
● Castle of three dragons (Zoological Museum)

Sculptures
● *Sorrow* by Josep Llimona
● *Lady with Parasol* by Joan Roig (1884) (in Zoo)
● *Homage to Picasso* by A Tàpies (1983) (on Passeig de Picasso)

In the 1860s and 1870s the great Citadel, a symbol of Bourbon oppression, was demolished. In its place, the city laid out its first public park, still a shady haven on the edge of the city hub.

The Citadel Covering an area almost as big as the city itself at the time, the monstrous Citadel was built to cow the Catalans after their defeat in 1714, by the new Bourbon monarch of Spain, Philip V. A garrison of 8,000 troops kept the population in check, and the Citadel was loathed as a place where local patriots were executed. In 1868, the Catalan General Juan Prim y Prats came to power and ordered its demolition, a process already begun by the citizens.

The park today The public park that took the Citadel's place (and name) shows little trace of the great fortress, though the Arsenal houses the Catalan Parliament. Other structures are leftovers from the Universal Expo of 1888: an ornate Arc de Triomf (Triumphal Arch), and a fairy-tale, *modernista* restaurant designed by Domènech i Montaner and now home to part of the Museum of Natural Sciences. The zoo is to the east (▷ 72), while the geology section of the Natural History Museum occupies a building on the southern flank. Throughout the park, fine trees and shrubs and a boating lake soften the formal layout. The imposing Cascada, an extraordinary fountain feature, incorporates just about every allegorical element possible and was worked on by Gaudí, then an architecture student.

The marina at Port Olímpic (left); stealing some shade at a café (right)

Port Olímpic and the Beaches

The eye-catching development of the Vila Olímpica, built for the 1992 Olympic Games, is a stunning ensemble of marinas, broad promenades, glittering buildings and open space.

Port Olímpic The marina is the heart of the new Olympic district, built as the focus of the water events, and backed by the apartments, which once housed the athletes. Sleek and expensive yachts and boats of all shapes and sizes line the pontoons. The enclosed marina, and the nearby promenades, are lined with bars and restaurants of all descriptions. Inland, the tallest buildings are the Mapfre towers and the opulent Hotel Arts, part of a development that had as big an impact on Barcelona as the 19th-century construction of the Eixample.

Fun in the sun To either side of Port Olímpic lie clean, sandy beaches, attracting both visitors and Barcelonins. The beaches stretch north from Barceloneta to the Forum complex (▷ 105), which was built to host a 'cultural olympics' in 2004. Spruced up in the late 1980s, the esplanade, 8km (5 miles) long, is backed by tree-lined grassy spaces, offering cyclists, roller-bladers and strollers an escape from the city. Along with water sports and beach games you'll find freshwater showers, sunbed rental, children's playparks and all you need for a day at the beach. When the sun sets there are the *chiringuitos* (beach bars) and restaurants in the Port Olímpic to refresh and revive.

THE BASICS

🚉 K9
✉ Port Olímpic
🚇 Ciutadella – Vila Olímpica
🚌 36, 45, 57, 59, 157

HIGHLIGHTS

● Frank Gehry's *Lobster* sculpture
● Strolling or cycling the Passeig Marítim
● El Fòrum (Forum complex)
● Sandy beaches

Port Vell

HIGHLIGHTS

● A meal or drink overlooking the marina
● Harbour trip on one of the *golondrinas* pleasure boats, www.lasgolondrinas.com
● The Aquàrium

TIPS

● Weekends there's a craft market near the Palau del Mar overlooking the Port Vell.
● Sundays are exceptionally busy, so watch your valuables.
● Shops in Maremagnum are open Sunday.

Renovations in the early 1990s reclaimed the Old Port and reintegrated it into city life. The modern Rambla de Mar walkway extends across the water to the Maremagnum complex, at the heart of the Old Port.

Back to the sea Barcelona has often been accused of ignoring the sea on which much of its prosperity depended. In the past, the closest most tourists came to it was an ascent of the 50m (165ft) Monument a Colom (commemorating the return of Columbus from the New World in 1493) at the seaward end of the Rambla. Now, Port Vell is given over to pleasure and entertainment and most shipping activity takes place at the modern port installations to the west, although ferries to the Balearics still depart from here.

Clockwise from left: the Rambla de Mar walkway; the Maremagnum complex at night and by day; the Aquàrium; one of the golondrine *pleasure boats*

Peninsula The Maremagnum, a huge covered shopping and entertainment complex at the heart of the Old Port, is connected to the mainland by the Rambla de Mar. This obelisk-lined walkway is usually thronged with tourists, but there are peaceful spots for a stroll. The area is particularly appealing in summer, when you want a sea breeze, and at night, when some of the restaurants and bars are worth checking out. After a major revamp, the shopping mall in the Maremagnum is now very good, while outside you'll find the Aquàrium, which is one of the largest in Europe and requires a couple of hours for a visit. Take a walk through the 80m long (265ft) glass tunnel with sharks a few inches from your face. Also worthwhile is the IMAX movie house. Barcelona's *golondrinas* (swallowboats) offer trips from the Port Vell quayside. Trips also tour the harbour and the coastline.

THE BASICS

Aquàrium
www.aquariumbcn.com
⊞ G9
⊠ Moll d'Espanya
☎ 93 221 74 74
🕐 Oct–May Mon–Fri 9.30–9, Sat, Sun 9.30–9.30; Jun, Sep daily 9.30–9.30; Jul, Aug daily 9.30am–11pm
🚇 Drassanes
🚌 14, 17, 36, 38, 40, 45, 57, 59, 64, 91, 157
💰 Expensive

Monument a Colom
⊞ F/G8
⊠ Plaça del Portal de la Pau
☎ 93 302 52 24
🕐 Currently closed to visitors
🚇 Barceloneta, Drassanes
🚌 14, 17, 36, 38, 40, 45, 57, 59, 64, 91
💰 Inexpensive

Santa Maria del Mar

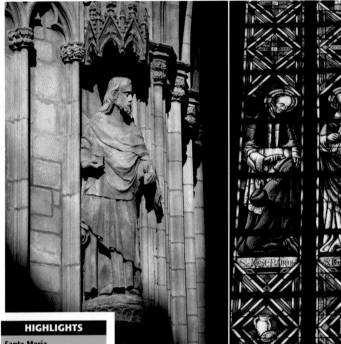

HIGHLIGHTS

Santa Maria
● Rose window in west front

In the Ribera
● Passeig del Born with central Rambla
● 19th-century glass-and-iron Born Market building
● Fosser de les Moreres square
● Medieval houses in Carrer Montcada

TIP

● The best time to visit is during the afternoon on a weekday, when there are fewer services.

A fortress of the faith in the old waterfront area of the Ribera, the Church of Our Lady of the Sea is one of the greatest expressions of Catalan Gothic. It was built on the proceeds of Barcelona's maritime supremacy in the Middle Ages.

The Ribera Literally 'the seaside' or 'waterfront', the Ribera was the city's hub in the 13th century, when Catalan commerce dominated the Western Mediterranean ports. Successful merchants and entrepreneurs set themselves up in fine town houses close to the busy shore, cheek by jowl with workers, dock porters and craftspeople. The street names of the Ribera still reflect the trades once practised here: Assaonadors (tanners), Espaseria (swordmaking), Argenteria (silversmithing) and Sombrerers (hatters).

A statue bathed in sunlight (left); detail of a stained-glass window (middle); the austere exterior of the church of Santa Maria del Mar (right)

People's church Santa Maria was begun in 1329, the foundation stone commemorating the Catalan conquest of Sardinia. Sometimes referred to as the Cathedral of the Ribera, Santa Maria has always been a popular church, the focus of this once busy port district; the whole population is supposed to have toiled on its construction for 50 years. The life of the Ribera was reflected in decorative touches such as delightful depictions of dock-workers on doors and the altar. The altar is crowned by a wooden model of a 15th-century ship. Other than that, the interior of the church is almost bare; its elaborate baroque furnishings were torched during the Civil War, though the glorious stained-glass windows survived. Now the calm and symmetry created by its high vaults and by the majestic spacing of its octagonal columns can be appreciated without distraction.

THE BASICS

✚ H8
✉ Plaça de Santa Maria
☎ 93 310 23 90
🕐 Mon–Sat 9–1.30, 4.30–8, Sun 10–1, 4.30–8
🚇 Jaume 1
🚌 14, 17, 36, 39, 45, 51, 57, 59, 64
♿ Good (near entrance)
👆 Free

More to See

DHUB MONTCADA

Part of the city's Design Hub, a museum dedicated to design in all its forms, DHUB Montcada offers a series of excellent temporary exhibitions. Recent exhibitions have explored everything from 3D printed objects to fashion photography. There is a café on the ground floor and a shop selling art books and designer knick-knacks.

✚ H8 ✉ Carrer Montcada 12 ☎ 93 256 23 00 🕐 Tue–Sat 11–7, Sun 11–5 💲 Moderate; free Sun after 3pm, 1st Sun of the month and for under 16s

MERCAT DEL BORN

www.mercatdelborn.org

This former covered market, closed since the 1970s, has reopened as a cultural centre featuring exhibitions, theatre and dance performances. The space was earmarked for a new library, but foundations of 18th-century Barcelona were discovered during building works and these have been magnificently preserved.

✚ H8 ✉ Plaça Comercial 12 🕐 Daily 🚇 Jaume 1

MUSEU DE LA XOCOLATA

www.museuxocolata.cat

A museum devoted to chocolate is bound to appeal to children. You'll find an overview of the history of chocolate from its New-World origins to its arrival in Europe. There are staggering chocolate creations and a tempting shop.

✚ H8 ✉ Carrer del Comerç 36 ☎ 93 268 78 78 🕐 Mon–Sat 10–7, Sun 10–3 🚇 Jaume 1 💲 Moderate

ZOO BARCELONA

www.zoobarcelona.cat

In the Parc de la Ciutadella (▷ 66), the zoo has more than 400 species, but its reputation lies in the primates. Most of the primates are in danger of extinction, most notably the Bornean orangutans and the mangabeys, the world's smallest monkey. Other fast-disappearing animals include the Iberian wolf and various big cats. Also a children's petting zoo.

✚ J8 ☎ 902 457 545 🕐 Jun–Sep daily 10–7; mid-Mar to May, Oct daily 10–6; Jan to mid-Mar, Nov, Dec daily 10–5 🚇 Barceloneta, Arc de Triomf 💲 Expensive

There are more than 400 species of animals at the Zoo Barcelona

La Ribera

You can experience the full range of the Born's architecture and soak up the atmosphere on this walk in the Ribera.

DISTANCE: 2km (1.2 miles) **ALLOW:** 60 minutes

START

PLAÇA DE SANTA MARIA DEL MAR
▷ 70 ✚ H8 🚇 Jaume I

1 Walk to the right of the Basilica de Santa Maria del Mar and continue onto Carrer de Santa Maria. Continue to the end to the back of the church.

2 Turn left, crossing over the Placeta de Montcada and into the Carrer de Montcada. At the end of Carrer de Montcada turn right onto Carrer de la Princesa.

3 Continue to the end of Carrer de la Princesa to Parc de la Ciutadella and Museu de Ciències Naturals. Turn right onto Passeig de Picasso and follow the perimeter of the park for one block.

4 Turn right onto Carrer de la Fusina and then left onto Carrer del Comerç. Here you walk around the facade of the former Mercat del Born (▷ 72).

END

PLAÇA DE SANTA MARIA DEL MAR
🚇 Jaume I

8 Turn right onto Carrer dels Canvis Vells. At the end of the road is the Plaça de Santa Maria del Mar.

7 Take Carrer del Bonaire out of the square, which further on changes its name to Carrer del Consolat de Mar. Stop when you reach the intersection with Carrer dels Canvis Vells on your right.

6 Turn left onto Carrer de Palau, which brings you to the charming Plaça de les Olles, a small square with outdoor cafés and apartment blocks with pretty facades.

5 With your back to the market, keep left, following Carrer del Comerç to the intersection with Avinguda del Marquès de l'Argentera.

Shopping

ALAMACEN MARABI

http://alamacenmarabi.
blogspot.com

These handmade felt toys aren't cheap, but their quality and sheer charm are priceless. Kids will love the large animals and teddy bears and there are smaller items, such as finger puppets, which make unique gifts.

+ H8 **✉** Flassaders 30bis **🚇** Jaume I

BARAKA

There is plenty to tempt you from Morocco in this small shop: handcrafted silver jewellery, brass lamps, *kilms* (woven rugs) and dainty *babuchas* (leather slippers).

+ H8 **✉** Carrer Canvis Vells 2 **☎** 93 268 42 20 **🚇** Jaume I, Barceloneta

BEATRIZ FUREST

Beatriz Furest's exquisitely designed bags and purses regularly feature on the pages of fashion magazines, yet manage to remain both stylish and timeless. A small selection of shoes, scarves and belts round out the line.

+ H8 **✉** Carrer Esparteria 1 **☎** 93 268 37 96 **🚇** Barceloneta, Jaume I

BUBÓ

Carles Mampel makes haute chocolate bonbons, cakes and other goodies, which he carefully displays in this chocolate 'boutique' with the reverence of fine jewellery. Next door there is a café where you can taste some before buying.

+ H8 **✉** Carrer Caputxes 10 **☎** 93 268 72 24 **🚇** Jaume I

CASA GISPERT

This establishment is an expert roaster of nuts and coffees, and sells everything from fresh-roasted hazelnuts and almonds to Iranian pistachios.

+ H8 **✉** Carrer de Sombrerers 23 **☎** 93 319 75 35 **🚇** Jaume I

LA COMERCIAL

Born is full of chic little shops selling designer goods for the home, but La Comercial is perhaps the most appealing. Whether you want a Diptyque candle, a trendy cushion or a fabulous rug, you're bound to find it here. Close by you will find five other branches of La Comercial, which contain men and women's fashion.

FINE DESIGN

Barcelona's design tradition and its endless array of unusual and individual shops make the hunt for gifts and accessories unusually enjoyable. Fine leather goods at reasonable prices can be found everywhere in the Eixample, and there are numerous expensive jewellery shops. In the Old Town, look for hand-painted jewellery, ceramics, textiles and crafts.

+ H8 **✉** Carrer Bonaire 4 **☎** 93 295 46 30 **🚇** Barceloneta, Jaume I

COMO AGUA DE MAYO

This lovely shop sells a select range of stylish yet highly feminine clothing from local designers. Names to watch out for include the bold prints of Ailanto and Josep Font's quirky, retro-inspired separates. Handmade shoes and accessories also.

+ H8 **✉** Carrer de Argenteria 43 **☎** 93 310 64 41 **🚇** Jaume I

DEMASIÉ

Cookie junkies will be in seventh heaven here. Mouth-watering treats in surprising flavours such as black chocolate and orange, Parmesan and Mallorcan sausage, boxed-up in pretty, fifties-style packaging that make great gifts.

+ H8 **✉** Carrer Princesa 28 **☎** 93 304 03 00 **🚇** Jaume I

GIDLÖÖF

This large, loft-style space contains a treasure trove of classic Scandinavian antiques and vintage goodies, lovingly restored by the owners. Classic designs, such as Mathsson chairs and metal bookcases by String, feature, along with their own furniture and textile collections.

+ H8 **✉** Passatge Mercantil 1, Born **☎** 93 368 22 25 **🚇** Barceloneta, Jaume I

IGUAPOP GALLERY

This hip, warehouse-like gallery specializes in graffiti and graphic artists, and top international names, such as Gary Baseman and Miss Kitten, are shown here. Part of the gallery incorporates a shop selling funky street and skate wear.

✚ H8 ✉ Carrer Comerç 15 ☎ 93 319 68 13 🚇 Jaume I

IVO & CO

This lovely emporium sells gifts and homewares from Provençal France: pottery, pretty dinnerware with floral motifs, spotted or striped tablecloths and tea towels, stationery and other knick-knacks. All items carry a distinct retro feel and some are genuine antiques.

✚ H8 ✉ Plaça del Comerç 3 ☎ 93 268 33 31 🚇 Jaume I

MAREMAGNUM

www.maremagnum.es
Best approached via the Rambla del Mar and the southwest entrance with a spectacular mirror canopy and a panoramic roof terrace, Maremagnum contains not only fashion boutiques, but also gift shops, cafés, restaurants, bars and nightspots.

✚ G9 ✉ Moll d'Espanya ☎ 93 225 81 00 🕐 Daily 10–10 🚇 Drassanes

MENCHÉN TOMÁS

Gorgeous frilly yet highly stylish women's wear with a distinctively French feel plus a range of delicate costume jewellery.

✚ H8 ✉ Carrer Rec 46 ☎ 93 310 64 69 🚇 Jaume I

MERCAT DE SANTA CATERINA

www.mercatsantacaterina.net
The range, variety and quality of the produce here reflects the area's wealth—this is one of Barcelona's most happening addresses—with everything from meat, fish and vegetables to flowers, imported groceries and luxury chocolates on offer.

✚ H7 ✉ Avinguda Francesc Cambò 16 ☎ 93 319 57 40 🚇 Jaume I

MINU MADHU

Come here for a superb range of shawls, scarves and elegant feminine silk jackets; scarves range from traditional Spanish fringed silk to pashminas, vibrant woollen wraps and lace and gossamer silk for evening wear.

SMALL OUTLETS

Catalonia was once known as a nation of shopkeepers and this is how most residents still shop: small outlets with personal service. Nobody seems to mind waiting for just the right cut of ham off the bone or a perfectly matching button. This sort of one-to-one contact is part of the experience for the visitor and all it takes is confidence in your communication skills.

✚ H8 ✉ Carrer de Santa Maria 18 ☎ 93 310 27 85 🚇 Jaume I

OLIVE

Everything in this long, narrow shop derives from the olive, from beautifully packaged soaps and body and bath products to bottles of olive oil from Spain, Italy and all over the Mediterranean. The gift sets make great souvenirs.

✚ H8 ✉ Plaça de les Olles 2 ☎ 93 310 58 83 🚇 Jaume I

ON LAND

Urban fashion for both men and women is *de rigeur* in Josep Abril's super-hip shop, which sells his own designs and labels such as Montse Ibañes and Petit Bateau; T-shirts by Divinas Palabras are a good buy.

✚ H8 ✉ Carrer de la Princesa 25 18 ☎ 93 310 02 11 🚇 Jaume I

VILA VINITECA

www.vilaviniteca.es
The number one shop for wine connoisseurs that supplies many of the city's top restaurants. The selection is so vast it is often overwhelming, but the staff is very helpful. As well as the staple tipples from La Rioja, seek out DOCs from the Priorat and Ribero del Duero. Their shop next door specializes in local gourmet produce.

✚ H8 ✉ Carrer Agullers 7 ☎ 90 232 77 77 🚇 Jaume I

Entertainment and Nightlife

C.D.L.C.

www.cdlcbarcelona.com
The nightspot of the see and be-seen crowd. It has Bedouin-style 'boudoirs' skirting the edge of the dance floor, two bars and a restaurant, right at the water's edge.
✚ J9 ✉ Passeig Marítim 32 ☎ 93 224 04 70 🕐 Daily noon–2.30am 🚇 Ciutadella–Vila Olímpica

CLUB SHÔKO

This elegant, Ibiza-style club by the sea appeals to a slightly older crowd by playing 80s funk during the week and house music on the weekends. It's best to get there before midnight if you want a prime spot on the lounge-terrace.
✚ J9 ✉ Passeig Marítim 36 ☎ 93 225 92 00 🕐 Daily midnight–3am 🚇 Cuitadella–Vila Olímpica

ECLIPSE

On the 26th floor of the W Hotel this smooth-as-silk bar has a staggering view of the coastline. DJs provide a cool soundtrack and the cocktail list is wildly imaginative. Try their signature vodka and passion fruit concoction.
✚ Off map G8 ✉ Plaça Rosa de les Vents ☎ 93 295 28 00 🕐 Sun–Thu 6pm–2am, Fri–Sat 6pm–3am 🚇 Barceloneta

GIMLET

The mixologists at this cool cocktail bar are the most professional around, and definitely know the difference between shaken and stirred. A smooth jazz soundtrack adds to the ambience.
✚ H8 ✉ Carrer Rec 24 ☎ 93 310 10 27 🕐 Mon–Sat 8pm–3am 🚇 Jaume 1

MAGIC CLUB

www.magic-club.net
One of the city's longest running rock clubs, Magic remains one of the only rock-themed discos in Barcelona. There are two dance floors and, as well as club nights, it also hosts live gigs by up-and-coming bands.
✚ H8 ✉ Passeig Picasso 40 ☎ 93 310 12 67 🕐 Thu–Sat and night before public hols 11pm–6am 🚇 Jaume I

PALAU DE LA MÚSICA CATALANA

www.palaumusica.org
Domènech i Montaner's Palace of Music has long been Barcelona's principal auditorium, a splendid setting for performances by European classical ensembles and visiting jazz artists. Reserve early.
✚ H7 ✉ Carrer Sant Francesc de Paula 2 ☎ 902 475 485 🚇 Urquinaona

RAZZMATAZZ

www.salarazzmatazz.com
Five nightclubs and top-notch live music venue (especially for indie and electronica) in one.
✚ K7 ✉ Carrer de Pamplona 88 ☎ 93 320 82 00 🕐 Fri and Sat 1am–6am 🚇 Bogatell

EL XAMPANYET

This traditional little bar can always be relied on for a lively crowd, good-value tapas and their specialty, a house cava. Seating at the small marble tables is limited, but the best place to sit is at the zinc bar.
✚ H8 ✉ Carrer Montcada 22 ☎ 93 319 70 03 🕐 Tue–Sat 12–4, 7–11 🚇 Jaume I

Restaurants

PRICES

Prices are approximate, based on a 3-course meal for one person.

€€€	over €50
€€	€25–€50
€	under €25

AGUA (€€)

Watch the waves while you eat at this modern, laid-back restaurant, where dishes range from modern, innovative starters to traditional Catalan fare. ➕ H/J9 ✉ Passeig Maritim de la Barceloneta 30 ☎ 93 225 12 72 🕙 Daily 🚇 Ciutadella Vila–Olímpica

ATRIL (€)

For bistro-style food at fair prices, this cosy eatery in the Sant Pere district is a good choice. The mussels and *pommes frites* are particularly good, though you are also likely to see couscous or *ceviche* (fish marinated in lime juice) on the international menu. Outdoor terrace and a great Sunday brunch. ➕ H7 ✉ Carrer Carders 23 ☎ 93 310 12 20 🕙 Closed Mon, 3 weeks in Aug 🚇 Jaume I

BESTIAL (€€)

Arguably the best seaside terrace in Barcelona, with wood decking and parasols, offering Italian fare at reasonable prices. ➕ J9 ✉ Carrer de Ramon Trias Fargas 2–4 ☎ 93

224 04 07 🕙 Daily 🚇 Ciutadella–Vila Olímpica

LA BOMBETA (€)

Most of the restaurants along the Passeig de Borbón, Barceloneta's main street, are incredibly touristy, so instead steer yourself to the side of this traditional tapas bar. The house specialty is *bombas*; giant, fluffy croquettes topped with a spicy *brava* sauce. Other dishes such as simply grilled prawns, squid and sardines, *pa amb tomà-quet* topped with *serrano* ham or cheese and Galician-style octopus are also incredibly tasty. ➕ H9 ✉ Carrer Maquinista 3 ☎ 93 319 94 45 🕙 Closed Wed 🚇 Barceloneta

EL CANGREJO LOCO (€€)

The crowds testify to the appeal of the reasonable prices on the *menú del día* of this large Port Olímpic seafood establishment.

FISH FOR ALL

The seafood restaurants of Barcelona, concentrated in bayside Barceloneta, are famous. They serve *zarsuela* (a seafood stew) and *suquet de peix* (fish-and-potato soup), as well as *fideus* (a paella-style dish with noodles instead of rice). *Arròs negre* is rice cooked in the black ink of a squid.

➕ K9 ✉ Moll de Gregal, Port Olímpic ☎ 93 221 17 48 🕙 Daily 🚇 Ciutadella–Vila Olímpica

CAN SOLÉ (€€)

Established in the early 1900s, this elegant old eating house is tiled and decorated with photos of former famous patrons. Join the regulars to enjoy superb paellas, sticky-fresh fish, lobsters and plates of sweet shrimp and prawns while watching the action in the frenetic open kitchen. ➕ H9 ✉ Carrer des Sant Carles 4 ☎ 93 221 50 12 🕙 Tue–Sat 1.30–4, 8.30–11, Sun 1.30–4 🚇 Barceloneta

CASA DELFÍN (€)

In the heart of El Born, Casa Delfín is as pretty as a picture, with a mezzanine floor, wooden furniture, quirky wall art and charming, retro elements. Catalan classics, such as *suquet* (fish stew), chickpeas and tripe and tomato and tuna belly salad are served, but Britannia rules in the dessert menu. If you are craving an Eton Mess or toffee pudding, here's your chance. ➕ H8 ✉ Passeig del Born 36 ☎ 93 319 50 88 🕙 Daily 🚇 Barceloneta, Jaume I

CENTRE CULTURAL EUSKAL ETXEA (€)

For authentic regional cooking, come and join the exiles from the Basque country at their

cultural hub, which serves an outstanding selection of *pintxos* (tapas) from this northern region. Expect superb seafood, tender octopus, Basque cheeses and smoked meats and sausages in a cozy, dark little bar.

➕ H8 ✉ Plaçeta de Montcada 1–3 ☎ 93 310 21 85 ◷ Daily 🚇 Jaume I

COMERÇ 24 (€€€)

Chef Carles Abellan trained with Ferran Adrià at El Bulli, and his sophisticated restaurant follows in the master's footsteps, serving up superb new wave Catalan cooking. Sample the *menú festival* to experience what this innovative cuisine is all about—and prepare to be amazed at the tastes, textures and combinations.

➕ H8 ✉ Carrer del Comerç 24 ☎ 93 319 21 02 ◷ Closed Sun and Mon 🚇 Arc de Triomf

KAIKU (€€)

Kaiku boasts a cosy maritime-themed interior and serves a surprisingly creative menu focusing on seafood. Come early to get a spot on its sought-after terrace by the beach. Dishes are prepared with carefully sourced produce, including their own organic vegetables and fish brought to the nearby dock, and include a fabulous paella made with smoked rice (*arròs a la xef*). They also do delicious desserts.

➕ Off map at H9 ✉ Plaça del Mar 1 ☎ 93 221 90 82 ◷ Tue–Sun 1–3.30, 7–11 🚇 Barceloneta

LITTLE ITALY (€€)

This restaurant is named after New York's Italian quarter and, although the chef is American, the food is not. The menu includes a range of pasta, meat and fish dishes, and there's a comprehensive wine list. A number of informal, comfortable rooms make up the dining space, and there is live jazz Tuesday, Wednesday, Thursday and Sunday nights.

➕ H8 ✉ Carrer del Rec 30 ☎ 93 319 79 73 ◷ Closed Sun 🚇 Barceloneta, Jaume 1

EL MAGATZEM DEL PORT (€€)

The grounds of Palau del Mar are home to five restaurants, all serving similar cuisine, but the small Harbour Warehouse

is known for its paellas and rice dishes. The restaurant presents a creative twist on traditional recipes and the chef seeks out all his ingredients at La Boqueria market, ensuring quality and freshness.

➕ H9 ✉ Palau del Mar, Plaça de Pau Vila ☎ 93 221 06 31 ◷ Closed Mon and Sun evening 🚇 Barceloneta

LA PARADETA (€€)

The form here is to buy a drink, inspect the mounds of mussels, clams, squid and crab and specify what you want, how you'd like it cooked and your choice of sauce. Then grab a seat at one of the refectory tables and wait till your number's called. Collect your plate and tuck in to enjoy some of the freshest and best seafood in Barcelona.

➕ H8 ✉ Carrer Comercial 7 ☎ 93 268 19 39 ◷ Lunch and dinner Tue–Sat, lunch only Sun, closed Mon 🚇 Arc de Triomf, Barceloneta

SET PORTES (€€€)

Founded in 1836, the 'Seven Doors' is one of Barcelona's most famous and reliable restaurants, serving up superb paella, fish and seafood. You can book for the 1.30–2.30 and the 8–9.30 slots; otherwise be prepared to wait.

➕ H8 ✉ Passeig d'Isabel II 14, Port Vell ☎ 93 319 30 33 ◷ Daily 🚇 Barceloneta

Largely built as the city expanded in the 19th century, L'Eixample (the extension) is a grid-patterned urban area, bisected by the arrow-straight Diagonal. It's home to the city's finest *modernista* buildings.

Casa Milà

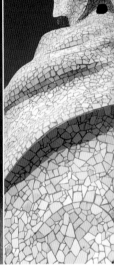

'Get a violin' was architect Gaudí's response to a resident who wondered where to install a grand piano in this coral reef of an apartment block, which seems designed for slithering sea creatures rather than human beings.

The grotto of the Passeig de Gràcia Anecdotes about the Casa Milà abound: the artist Santiago Rusinyol is supposed to have said that a snake would be a more suitable pet here than a dog. Lampooned for decades after its completion in 1912, this extraordinary building has been rescued from neglect and opened to visitors. Nicknamed La Pedrera (stone quarry), it was built for Pere Milà Camps, a rich industrialist who afterward complained that Gaudí's extravagance had reduced him to penury. The steel frame that

Clockwise from left: the dramatic staircase in the Casa Milà; close-up detail of an elaborate chimney; the facade; clusters of other chimney designs

supports the seven-floor structure is completely concealed behind an undulating outer skin of stone bedecked with balconies whose encrustations of ironwork resemble floating fronds of seaweed. Obscured from the street, the rooftop undulates too, and is scattered with clusters of centurion-like chimneys.

One of Gaudí's greatest Gaudí originally proposed a spiral ramp that would bring automobiles to the apartment doors—an impractical idea as it turned out—but the Casa Milà nevertheless had one of the world's first underground garages. The building's beautifully brick-vaulted attics have become the Espai Gaudí, the best place to learn about Gaudí's life and work. Of particular interest are the interior photographs of some of the Gaudí buildings that are not normally open to the public.

THE BASICS

www.lapedrera.com

🛨 G5

✉ Provença 261–265

☎ 90 240 09 73

🕐 Mar–Oct 9–8; Nov–Feb 9–6.30. Last admission half an hour before closing. Closed 1 and 6–14 Jan, 25–26 Dec

🚇 Diagonal

🚌 7, 16, 17, 22, 24, 28

♿ Good (but not on roof)

💷 Expensive

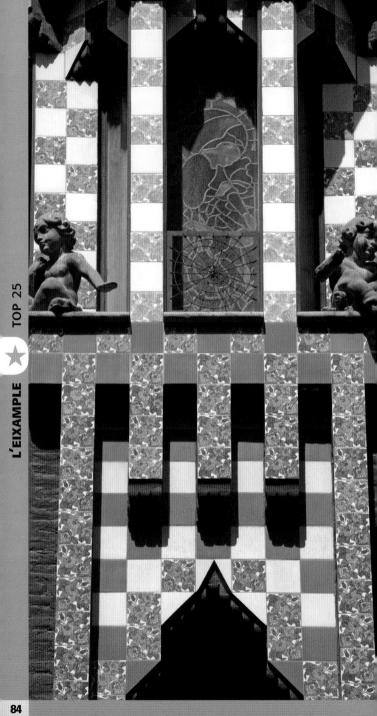

Casa Vicens (opposite); relaxing in the shade (left) and sun (right)

Gràcia

This distinctive neighbourhood is the site of the Park Güell and a genuine Gaudí masterpiece. You'll find peaceful squares, lively bars and a seven-day street party attracting more than 1.5 million each year.

Cultural village Originally a collection of tiny farms, Gràcia grew rapidly in the 19th century, becoming part of Barcelona itself in 1897. Gràcia was renowned then as a cultural and political hub, and this is reflected in some street names— Mercat de la Libertat and Plaça de la Revolució. It was also a place where music and theatre thrived and today there are exhibition areas, music societies and cultural spaces of all kinds.

Graceful Gràcia Apart from the Park Güell (▷ 88–89), the pick of Gràcia attractions are Gaudí's exquisite Casa Vicens, one of the world's first *modernista* buildings, and Lluis Domènech i Montaner's Casa Fuster, which has been converted to a hotel. *Plaças* such as Virreina, Sol and Vila de Gràcia are attractive places to pause or stop for a coffee during the day. Boasting some of the best bars and restaurants in the city, Gràcia comes into its own at night.

Summer festival The *Festa Major* has taken place annually for more than 150 years. For seven days during the second half of August, it takes over Gràcia. Each street puts up a display, with themes ranging from the Wild West to the Civil War, and the suburb is a riot of colour. You'll also find music and plays peformed outdoors on the various *plaças*.

THE BASICS

⊞ G/H4
🍴 Many restaurants and bars
🚇 Fontana, Gràcia, Joanic
🚌 22, 24, 28, 39, 55

HIGHLIGHTS

Casa Vicens
● Elaborate exterior decoration
● Decorative wrought-iron gates

Casa Fuster
● Mix of neo-Gothic and classical styles
● Viennese-style ground floor café

Plaça de la Vila de Gràcia
● Bell tower, designed by Antoni Rovira i Trias

Park Güell
● Incredible tilework
● Amazing city views

TOP 25

Manzana de la Discòrdia

HIGHLIGHTS

No. 35
● Exterior sculptures
● Dome perched on columns

No. 41
● Sculpture of St. George and dragon by entrance
● Grotesque sculptures in third-floor windows
● Lamps and stained-glass panels in entrance

No. 43
● Chromatic designs on facade by Gaudí's collaborator, the artist Josep Maria Jujol

TIP

● The Casa Batlló is hugely popular in the mornings. Go late afternoon for a less-crowded visit.

A century ago, the bourgeoisie of Barcelona vied with each other in commissioning ever more extravagant homes. The most extraordinary of these ornament the Block of Discord on Passeig de Gràcia.

Enlivening the Eixample In an attempt to relieve the rigidity of Cerdà's grid of streets, *modernista* architects studded the Eixample with some of the most exciting urban buildings ever seen. *Modernisme*, the uniquely Catalan contribution to late 19th-century architecture, has obvious links with art nouveau, but here it also breathes the spirit of nationalism and civic pride because Barcelona was the richest city in Spain. The Manzana de la Discòrdia juxtaposes the work of three great architects of the age.

Clockwise from left: the glittering facade and curved staircase at Casa Batlló; the splendid St. George and Dragon sculpture on the facade of Casa Amatller; the wedding cake on top of Casa Lleó-Morera; balcony detail, Casa Batlló

THE BASICS

www.casabatllo.es
www.amatller.org
✚ G6
✉ Passeig de Gràcia 35, 41, 43
☎ Casa Batlló: 93 216 03 06; Casa Amatller: 93 487 72 17
🕐 Casa Batlló: daily 9–9, last admission 8pm; Casa Amatller: guided tours Sat (reservations essential—tel 670 466 260 or email casessingulars @casessingulars.com)
Ⓜ Passeig de Gràcia
🚌 7, 16, 17, 22, 24, 28
♿ Fair
💷 Expensive

No. 35 Domènech i Montaner completed the six-floor Casa Lleó-Morera in 1905. Much of this corner building was destroyed during improvements in the 1940s, but its striking *modernista* style and curved balconies have survived.

No. 41 Built in 1898 by Puig i Cadafalch (currently under restoration) the Casa Amatller has an internal courtyard and staircase like the medieval palaces along Carrer Montcada. Outside, it is a wonderful mixture of Catalan Gothic and Flemish Renaissance, faced with bright tiles and topped by a big gable.

No. 43 The Casa Batlló reflects the hand of Antoni Gaudí, who restyled the house in 1906. It is said to represent the triumph of St. George over the dragon with its heaving roof, scaly skin of mosaic tiles, windows and tower.

Park Güell

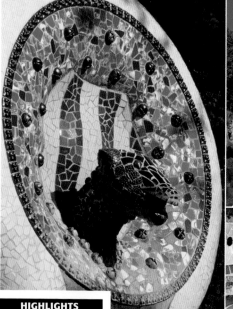

HIGHLIGHTS

● Dragon at entrance to park
● Curved and tiled benches on main square
● Entrance pavilions
● Ironwork of entrance gates
● Palm-like stonework of buttresses
● Leaning pillars of arcade
● *Modernista* furnishings in Casa Museu Gaudí

TIP

● The metro is 15 minutes' uphill walk from the park (assisted by escalators) and the only bus that stops outside is the No. 24; use the Bus Turístic if you have a ticket.

Surrealist Salvador Dalí was filled with 'unforgettable anguish' as he strolled among the uncanny architectural forms of this hilltop park, Antoni Gaudí's extraordinary piece of landscape design.

Unfulfilled intentions The rocky ridge, which has a magnificent view of Barcelona and the Mediterranean, was bought in 1895 by Gaudí's rich patron, Eusebi Güell, with the idea of developing an English-style garden city (hence the British spelling of 'park'. The project flopped; only three houses of the proposed 60 were built, and the area was taken over by the city council as a park in 1923.

Anatomy of a park The main feature is the great terrace, supported on a forest of neo-

Animal mosaic (left); the main staircase (top middle); the swirls of benches in the Gran Plaça (bottom middle); the Sala Hipóstila (right)

Grecian columns and bounded by a sinuous balustrade-cum-bench whose form was allegedly copied from the imprint left by a human body in a bed of plaster; the surface is covered by fragments of bright ceramic tiles. The strange space beneath the terrace was intended to be a market; it gapes cavernlike at the top of the steps leading from the park's main entrance.

Surreal landscape A ceramic serpent (or perhaps a dragon) slithers down the stairway toward the main entrance, which is guarded by two gingerbread-style buildings with bulbous roofs that must be among Gaudí's oddest creations. Gaudí scattered the park with other idiosyncratic details, steps and serpentine paths. In his later years he lived in the house built by his pupil Berenguer, now the Casa Museu Gaudí.

THE BASICS

✚ H/J2
✉ Carrer d'Olot
☎ 93 213 04 88
🕐 Park: May–Sep daily 10–9; Apr, Oct 10–8; Mar, Nov 10–7; Dec–Feb 10–6. Casa Museu Gaudí and Centre d'Interpretació: Apr–Sep daily 10–8; Oct–Mar 10–6
🍴 Café
🚇 Lesseps
🚌 24, 87
♿ Few
🎫 Park: free

Sagrada Família

George Orwell thought Gaudí's great Temple of the Holy Family one of the ugliest buildings he ever saw, and wondered why the Anarchists hadn't wrecked it in the Civil War. Today it is an emblem of the city.

Devoted designer A must on every visitor's itinerary, Barcelona's most famous building is a mere fragment of what its architect intended. The ultrapious Gaudí began work in 1883, and for the latter part of his life dedicated himself utterly to building a temple that would do penance for the materialism of the modern world. There was never any expectation that the great structure would be completed in his lifetime; his plan called for 18 high towers dominated by an even taller one, an amazing 170m (560ft) high, dedicated to

Jesus Christ. What he did succeed in completing was one of the towers, the major part of the east (Nativity) front, the pinnacled apse and the crypt, where he camped out during the last months of his life before he was run down and killed by a tram. Ever since, the fate of the building has been the subject of sometimes bitter controversy.

Work in progress Many Barcelonins would have preferred the church to be left as it was at Gaudí's death, a monument to its creator. During the Civil War the Anarchists destroyed Gaudí's models and drawings though they spared the building. But enthusiasm for completion of the project was revived in the 1950s. Work has continued, though opponents believe that attempting to reproduce Gaudí's unique forms in modern materials can only lead to the creation of pastiche.

THE BASICS

www.sagradafamilia.org

🔡 J5

✉ Mallorca 401 (entrance on Carrer Sardenya)

☎ 93 208 04 14

🕐 Apr–Sep daily 9–8; Oct–Mar 9–6. Open 9–2 on 25–26 Dec, 1 and 6 Jan

🚇 Sagrada Família

🚌 10, 19, 33, 34, 43, 44, 50, 51

💷 Expensive

More to See

DISSENY HUB

www.dhub-bcn.cat

The city's newest, shiniest museum is dedicated to design, and occupies a striking contemporary building which overlooks the Plaça de les Glòries. Opening in 2014, the Disseny Hub (Design Hub) museum will cover all aspects of design, with collections of textiles, ceramics and decorative arts, and excellent temporary exhibitions. ✚ K6 ✉ Plaça de les Glòries s/n ⊕ See website for opening times ⊕ Glòries

FUNDACIÓ ANTONI TÀPIES

Joan Miró's mantle as the Grand Old Man of Catalan art was convincingly worn by Tàpies, who died in 2012. His earthy creations can be seen in this magnificently restored *modernista* building by Domènech i Montaner. It is topped with Tàpies' rooftop sculpture *Cloud and Chair*, an extraordinary extrusion of wire and tubing. ✚ G6 ✉ Carrer d'Aragó 255 ☎ 93 487 03 15 ⊕ Tue–Sun 10–8 ⊕ Passeig de Gràcia ⊕ Good ⊕ Moderate

HOSPITAL DE LA SANTA CREU I SANT PAU

Disliking the monotony of the Eixample, Domènech i Montaner deliberately defied it by aligning the buildings of Barcelona's first modern hospital at 45 degrees to its grid of streets. It was laid out like a self-contained village with patients housed in 48 separate pavilions. The medical facilities have been moved to modern premises, and the complex is currently under restoration, but can still be viewed by tour. ✚ K4 ✉ Carrer de Sant Antoni Maria Claret 167 ☎ 699 403 729 ⊕ Daily 10.15 and 12.15 ⊕ Sant Pau Dos de Maig ⊕ Expensive

TORRE AGBAR

Designed by French architect Jean Nouvel, the striking bullet-shaped Torre Agbar is an example of the city's new breed of architecture. At night a second aluminium skin reflects blue, green and red lights, which shine through a series of slats, creating a water-like, rippling effect visible all over the Eixample area. ✚ L6 ✉ Plaça de les Glòries s/n ⊕ Glòries

Fundació Antoni Tàpies

Facade of the Hospital de la Santa Creu i Sant Pau

L'Eixample

A walk that combines some fine *modernista* architecture with a stroll down one of the Eixample's major shopping thoroughfares.

DISTANCE: 2km (1.2 miles)   **ALLOW:** 50 minutes

START

PLAÇA JOAN CARLES I
🚇 G5 🚇 Diagonal

❶ The first part of this walk assumes you have already seen the Casa Milà (▷ 82–83) and the Manzana de la Discòrdia (▷ 86–87) and leads you past some of the lesser-known *modernista* buildings of the Eixample. Walk eastward along the Diagonal, which cuts through the area.

❷ Turn right onto Carrer de Roger de Llúria, then turn left onto Carrer de València to the medieval church and the market of La Concepció. The church was brought here piece by piece from its original site in the old town in the 19th century.

❸ Retrace your steps to Carrer de Roger de Llúria and turn left. Continue ahead and turn right onto Carrer d'Aragó.

END

PLAÇA DE CATALUNYA
▷ 50 🚇 G7 🚇 Catalunya

❻ Turn left to follow the central pedestrian promenade of Rambla de Catalunya to Plaça de Catalunya, the city's central square (▷ 50).

❺ Stay on the south side of Aragó to see the rooftop sculpture, *Cloud and Chair*, of the Fundació Antoni Tàpies.

❹ The crossing with Passeig de Gràcia gives you another chance to admire the incredible extravagances of the Manzana de la Discòrdia and to take in anything you missed first time round.

Shopping

ADOLFO DOMÍNGUEZ

One of Spain's brightest fashion stars, Domínguez's clothes for men and women manage to be mature yet achingly stylish. His 'U' range caters to a more urban look.
⊞ G6 ✉ Passeig de Gràcia 32 (and at other locations in the city hub) ☎ 93 487 41 70 Ⓜ Passeig de Gràcia

ALTAÏR

A profusion of books and maps on destinations worldwide, including Barcelona, Catalonia and Spain.
⊞ G6 ✉ Gran Vía de les Corts Catalans 616 ☎ 93 342 71 71 Ⓜ Passeig de Gràcia

ANTONIO MIRO

The first Catalan to make a name for himself in the world of fashion, Miro's men's and women's wear has remained timelessly stylish and beautifully tailored.
⊞ G6 ✉ Carrer Consell de Cent 349 ☎ 93 487 06 70 Ⓜ Passeig de Gràcia

ARMAND BASI

Basi is one of Spain's best-known designers and you'll find his range for both men and women at this flagship store.
⊞ G6 ✉ Passeig de Gràcia 49 ☎ 93 215 14 21 Ⓜ Passeig de Gràcia

BAGUÉS

Located on the ground floor of the Casa Amatller (▷ 87), this sumptuous jewellery shop has been serving the good ladies of the Eixample for over 250 years. Its constantly changing collections, in which many pieces are inspired by art nouveau motifs, don't come cheap—but their sheer exquisiteness is worth every euro.
⊞ G6 ✉ Passeig de Gràcia 41 ☎ 93 216 01 73 Ⓜ Passeig de Gràcia

BCN BOOKS

This bookshop has a good selection of classics and modern fiction from around the world in English.
⊞ H5 ✉ Roger de Llúria 118 ☎ 93 457 76 92 Ⓜ Diagonal

BULEVARD DELS ANTIQUARIS

Every kind of antiques dealer can be found in this complex of more than 70 shops next to the Bulevard Rosa mall.
⊞ G6 ✉ Passeig de

SERIOUS SHOPPING
The L'Eixample is Barcelona's serious shopping district, with the Passeig de Gràcia its jewel in the crown. This elegant avenue boasts the most expensive retail real estate in Spain, and its residents reflect this. Names such as Dolce and Gabbana and Gucci are at the northern end, while homegrown designers congregate in the south. Check out the cross-streets, too.

Gràcia 55 ☎ 93 215 44 99 Ⓜ Passeig de Gràcia

BULEVARD ROSA

Boasts 100-plus boutiques with the best in fashion, shoes and accessories.
⊞ G6 ✉ Passeig de Gràcia 53–5 ☎ 93 215 83 31 Ⓜ Passeig de Gràcia

CAMPER

This Mallorca-based shoe brand, famous for mixing quirky style with comfort, has shops and outlets all over the city. But this shop, in the Triangle shopping centre, has one of the largest ranges.
⊞ G7 ✉ Carrer Pelai 13–37 ☎ 93 302 41 24 Ⓜ Catalunya

COLMADO QUILEZ

One of Barcelona's great food stores still retains its old mirrors and ceiling-high shelves, which are stacked with a superb variety of groceries, cheeses, hams and alcohol of every description. Saffron, anchovies and coffee are sold in beautiful packaging under Quilez' own label—as is caviar, if you really want to push the boat out.
⊞ G6 ✉ Rambla de Catalunya 63 ☎ 93 215 23 56 Ⓜ Passeig de Gràcia

DESIGUAL

The bright and funky streetwear from a re-madeover Spanish label is causing a stir for its quirky designs and

unusual prints.

➕ G6 ✉ Passeig de Gràcia 47 ☎ 93 304 31 64 🚇 Passeig de Gràcia

DOLORES PROMESAS

www.dolorespromesas.com

Dolores Promesas specializes in gorgeous fashion with a playful twist for women, and their flagship store here boasts a wonderful range of flirty dresses and playsuits with a vintage feel, as well as fun T-shirts and leisure wear.

➕ G5 ✉ Rambla Catalunya 111 ☎ 93 496 04 61 🚇 Diagonal

ELS ENCANTS FLEA MARKET

Patient searching can reveal gold among the worn clothing, broken furniture and other unwanted items. Visit early for the best choice.

➕ K6 ✉ Plaça de les Glòries ☎ 93 246 30 30 🕐 Mon, Wed, Fri, Sat 7am–9pm 🚇 Glòries

L'ILLA

One of the city's larger and better *centro comerciales* with loads of fashion, electronic and homeware shops, a supermarket and an extensive food court.

➕ Off map ✉ Diagonal 555 🚌 6, 7, 30, 33, 34, 66, 67, 68

JOSEP FONT

Beloved by women for his feminine lines, innovative, stand-alone design and extraordinary eye for fabrics.

➕ G5 ✉ Carrer de Provença 304 ☎ 93 487 21 10 🚇 Passeig de Gràcia

MANGO

International chain of women's fashion stores with attractive, well-made clothes at affordable prices. Other branches in the central hub.

➕ G6 ✉ Passeig de Gràcia 65 ☎ 93 215 75 30 🚇 Passeig de Gràcia

MASSIMO DUTTI

Natty designs at more than reasonable prices in this nationwide outlet. Shirts a specialty.

➕ G4 ✉ Via Augusta 33 ☎ 93 217 73 06 🚇 Gràcia (FGC)

SANTA EULÀLIA

This prestigious emporium sells a selection of international luxury labels, such as Dior, Prada and Marc Jacobs. They also have a bespoke tailoring service.

➕ G5 ✉ Passeig de Gràcia 91 ☎ 93 215 42 24 🚇 Diagonal

OUTLET FEVER

You'll find plenty of shops claiming to be 'outlet' in Barcelona, but very few are actually the real thing. Exceptions are the clutch of shops along the Carrer Girona between the Gran Via and Carrer Casp. Here are fashion labels such as Mango, Nice Day and Etxart & Panno at greatly reduced prices.

SEPHORA

www.sephora.es

This French company came up with the brilliant idea of selling top-of-the-range cosmetics and scents on supermarket merchandising principles and have never looked back. Competitively priced products are ranged in order round the store, while assistants are on hand to offer samples and advice—customers are welcome to experiment.

➕ G7 ✉ El Triangle, Carrer Pelai 13–39 ☎ 93 306 39 00 🚇 Catalunya

TOUS

This costume jewellery and leatherwear company is known the world over. They made their mark with their iconic range of accessories featuring a teddy bear motif, but have expanded to more sophisticated pieces.

➕ G5 ✉ Passeig de Gràcia 75 ☎ 93 488 15 58 🚇 Diagonal, Passeig de Gràcia

VINÇON

www.vincon.com

This emporium is closely tied to the city's vibrant design culture. Over the decades the owner has pioneered homegrown talent, often by promoting their work in imaginative window displays. Products cover homewares, plus bags, watches and smaller items.

➕ G5 ✉ Passeig de Gràcia 96 ☎ 93 215 60 50 🚇 Diagonal

Entertainment and Nightlife

ANTILLA BARCELONA

The best of salsa and merengue—guaranteed good times and free dance lessons to get you going.

🞤 F6 ✉ Carrer d'Aragó 141–143 ☎ 93 451 21 51 🕐 Wed–Sat 11pm–5am, Sun 7pm–2am 🚇 Hospital Clinic

BIKINI

A large club in the L'Illa shopping mall, with separate spaces for cocktails, salsa and rock.

🞤 Off map ✉ Déu I Mata 105 ☎ 93 322 08 00 🕐 Closed Mon, Tue 🚇 Les Corts

CITY HALL

Three different levels blast out a range of music spanning techno to deep-house, while lounging night owls chill out on the terrace. One of downtown Barca's best places for dancing the night away.

🞤 G6 ✉ Rambla de Catalunya 2–4 ☎ 93 317 21 77 🕐 Daily midnight–5am 🚇 Catalunya

DRY MARTINI

This elegant, ocean liner-style cocktail bar serves the best martinis in town.

🞤 F5 ✉ Carrer d'Aribau 162–166 ☎ 93 217 50 72 🕐 Daily until 2.30am 🚇 Provença, Hospital Clínic, Diagonal

LES GENS QUE J'AIME

This basement bar has authentic Parisian *fin de siècle* touches, and is the perfect spot for an intimate cocktail on one of the velvet settees.

🞤 H5 ✉ Carrer Valencia 286 ☎ 93 215 68 79 🕐 Daily until 2.30am 🚇 Diagonal

HOTEL OMM

Naturally, the city's most design-conscious hotel has its trendiest club and bar. Omm Sessions whooshes into cheek-kissing action in the hotel's basement, while live music can be enjoyed at Omm Sessions in the chic lobby bar (Wed 8.30).

🞤 G5 ✉ Carrer Roselló 265 ☎ 93 445 40 00 🕐 Wed–Sat 11.30pm–3.30am 🚇 Diagonal

LUZ DE GAS

It's worth the journey to party and listen to good music in this splendidly restored old music hall, which varies its live acts. Jazz and blues bands grace the stage early in the week, giving way to rock, funk and Latin music on the weekends.

🞤 F3 ✉ Carrer de Muntaner 246 ☎ 93 209 77 11 🚇 Muntaner (FGC)

QUIET PLEASE

Stringent new laws on noise are playing havoc with the city's nightlife. Many bars and clubs are having to close, either permanently or while they soundproof their venues, or move to less residential spots. Revellers are asked to do their bit by keeping their voices down while waiting in line or leaving a bar.

OTTO ZUTZ

This club is still the place to see and be seen for Barcelona's glitterati and those aspiring to join them. Clever lighting and metal staircases and galleries set the scene.

🞤 G4 ✉ Carrer de Lincoln 15 ☎ 93 238 07 22 🕐 Wed–Sat 🚇 Gràcia

TEATRE NACIONAL DE CATALUNYA

Catalonia's official public playhouse has its own resident company. Famous Spanish and international productions are staged.

🞤 Off map ✉ Plaça de les Arts 1 ☎ 93 306 57 00 🚇 Glóries

VINITO

This wine-shop-cum-bar offers an excellent choice of wines by the glass, along with a simple selection of *montaditos* (slices of French bread with different tapas). You can also try *vermut*, poured straight from the barrel.

🞤 Off map ✉ Déu I Mata 105 ☎ 93 322 08 00 🕐 Closed Mon, Tue 🚇 Les Corts

XIX

This unassuming bar has a USP: the best gin and tonics in town expertly mixed by a Scottish barman. You'll be lucky to get one of the small tables, though a terrace provides extra seating.

🞤 E8 ✉ Carrer Rocafort 19 ☎ 93 423 43 14 🕐 Closed Sun 🚇 Rocafort

Restaurants

ALKIMIA (€€€)

The stark, minimal dining room can be a little sober, but it's the food that matters here. Chef Jordi Vilà's brilliant cooking has won the hearts of Barcelona's foodies.
🕂 J4/5 ✉ Carrer de la Indústria 79 ☎ 93 207 61 15 🕔 Closed Sat, Sun, 3 weeks in Aug 🚇 Sagrada Família

EL ASADOR DE BURGOS (€€€)

For a taste of the meat-heavy northern Spanish diet head for this traditional Castilian grill house, where whole suckling pigs, tender within and crackling without, and racks of lamb are roasted in the wood-fired oven. Other choices include sausages, superb ham and choice morsels of offal, with good house wine if you don't want to pay the high prices for others on the list.
🕂 H5 ✉ Carrer del Bruc 118 ☎ 93 207 31 60 🕔 Closed Sun dinner 🚇 Verdaguer

BOTAFUMEIRO (€€€)

This spacious Galician restaurant on Gràcia's main street serves delicious shellfish and a selection of seafood from the Atlantic coast.
🕂 G4 ✉ Gran de Gràcia 81, Gràcia ☎ 93 218 42 30 🕔 Daily 🚇 Fontana

CACAO SAMPAKA (€)

A small chain specializing in haute cuisine chocolate sold in stylish packaging and unusual tastes. There is a rear café, where the hot chocolate is on tap and sandwiches and cakes are delicious. It's great for a late breakfast, or a calorie-ridden afternoon tea after shopping.
🕂 G6 ✉ Carrer Consell de Cent 292 ☎ 93 272 08 33 🕔 Closed Sun 🚇 Passeig de Gràcia

CASA CALVET (€€€)

This beautiful, modern restaurant is housed in a Gaudí building and specializes in cutting-edge Catalan cuisine. The

service and ambience are all you would expect in a top-class establishment.
🕂 H6 ✉ Carrer de Casp 48 ☎ 93 412 40 12 🕔 Closed Sun 🚇 Urquinaona

CERVECERIA CATALANA (€)

It's generally agreed that the Cerveceria Catalana serves the best tapas in town, so getting a table here can often require patience (they don't take bookings). Instead grab a seat at the bar and peruse their mouthwatering array of morsels.
🕂 G5 ✉ Carrer Mallorca 236 ☎ 93 216 03 68 🕔 Daily 🚇 Passeig de Gracia

CHIDO ONE (€)

Crammed full of Mexican kitsch and tequila bottles, the authentic dishes here include mouth-puckering *ceviches*, huge *burritos*, gusty *mole* sauces and vats of fiery *salsa*.
🕂 H4 ✉ Carrer de Torrijos 30 ☎ 93 285 03 35 🕔 Mon–Fri 7pm–2am, Sat, Sun 1pm–2am 🚇 Fontana

CINC SENTITS (€€€)

Ingredients sourced from all over the world are lovingly and inspirationally combined at this cutting-edge restaurant, the 'Five Senses'. Dishes, which are served as part of a 6- or 8-course tasting menu, range from simple grills with a twist to slow-cooked braises with imaginative vegetable pairings.

Puddings are light or rich, whichever you fancy, and the wine list is extensive.
🔶 F6 ✉ Carrer d'Aribau 58 ☎ 93 323 94 90 🕐 Tue–Sat 1.30–3.30, 8.30–11
🚇 Passeig de Gràcia

CIUDAD CONDAL (€)

This modern tapas restaurant has a summer terrace. Go for classics like Spanish omelette or *tapas bravas*, or more creative fare like Basque spider crab or slivers of fried artichokes.
🔶 G6 ✉ Rambla de Catalunya 18 ☎ 93 318 19 97 🕐 Daily 8am–1.30am
🚇 Catalunya

CORNELIA & CO (€)

This large deli-café offers a bit of everything: freshly made pasta and cakes, gourmet bread and sandwiches, sushi and oysters. There is an ample selection of products to take away. It's a lovely option for breakfast or brunch.
🔶 G5 ✉ Carrer Valencia 225 ☎ 93 272 39 56 🕐 Daily from 9am
🚇 Passeig de Gràcia

EMBAT (€€)

This cosy place is understated but it's big among the city's gastro set. Lunches are good value—you may eat wild mushroom cannelloni or poached eggs with chorizo, depending on the season. At night, a tasting menu may consist of four tapas-sized courses and a pair of mouth-watering desserts.
🔶 J5 ✉ Carrer Mallorca 304 ☎ 93 458 08 55
🕐 Closed Sun, Mon, Wed dinner 🚇 Verdaguer

IKIBANA (€€)

A fashionable restaurant specializing in Brazilian-Japanese fusion cuisine, Ikibana also has an outdoor terrace and a trendy bar. The menu changes according to what is in season, but always includes some creative sushi, fresh seafood dishes, and unusual desserts. There's another branch in the Born.
🔶 H5 ✉ Avinguda del Parallel 148 ☎ 93 177 07 42
🕐 Daily 1.30–4, 8.30–2.30am
🚇 Poble Sec

JAUME DE PROVENÇA (€€€)

Interesting international dishes vary a menu of Catalan specialties, all prepared with refinement

---

SPECIAL TODAY

Many local people make lunch the main meal of the day and eat relatively frugally in the evening. One reason for following their example is to benefit from the bargain represented by the *menú del día* (fixed-price menu). It is likely to consist of three courses plus bread and a drink, a combination that would cost considerably more if the dishes were selected individually, particularly in the evening.

---

by acclaimed local chef Jaume Bargués.
🔶 E5 ✉ Carrer de Provença 88 ☎ 93 430 00 29 🕐 Closed Mon, Sun
🚇 Entença

MOO (€€€)

The ultra trendy Omm Hotel hosts Moo, one of the city's most talked-about restaurants. Run by the Michelin-starred Roca Brothers, the best way to taste their quirky, molecular cookery is with a tasting menu. Finish with a dessert inspired by a famous perfume.
🔶 G5 ✉ Carrer Rosselló 265 ☎ 93 445 40 00
🕐 Closed Sun 🚇 Diagonal

L'OLIVÉ (€€)

Good service and delicious Catalan meat and seafood dishes in a traditional setting.
🔶 G6 ✉ Carrer de Balmes 47 ☎ 93 452 19 90 🕐 Closed Sun evening
🚇 Universitat

PACO MERALGO (€€)

Scandi-style long benches and high stools adorn this upmarket tapas bar, where you can enjoy classics such as oven-baked clams, home-made *empanadillas* (small pies) and more substantial fare such as Mediterranean rice dishes and stews. The wine list is equally good.
🔶 Off map ✉ Carrer Muntaner 171 ☎ 93 430 90 27 🕐 Daily 1.30–4, 8.30–2.30am 🚇 Poble Sec

Around the central city, there's a clutch of sights that combine Barcelona's history with its present-day preoccupations. Pedralbes gives an insight into the medieval world and grand early-20th-century living, while Tibidabo and Nou Camp represent its modern pleasures.

Parc de
les Heures

B-20

RONDA DE DALT

RONDA DE DALT

Parc de la
Guineueta

Parc de la
Creueta
del Coll

Parc del Turó
de la Peira

Park
Güell

TÚNEL DE LA ROVIRA

Parc del
Guinardó

TRAVESSERA DE DALT

GRÀCIA

RONDA DEL GUINARDÓ

Parc de
les Aigües

AVINGUDA MERIDIANA

Parc
Pegaso

SAGRADA
FAMÍLIA

AVINGUDA DIAGONAL

CARRER D'ARAGÓ

MPLE

Parc
del Clot

VIA DE LES CORTS CATALANES

C-3

AVINGUDA MERIDIANA

Parc Estació
del Nord

AVINGUDA DIAGONAL

LA RIBERA

PASSEIG DE PICASSO

CARRER DE LA MARINA

Parc
de la
Ciutadella

Parc
Diagonal
Mar

RONDA LITORAL

Parc del
Poblenou

B-10

El Fòrum

PORT
OLÍMPIC

0   1 km

0   1 mile

Museu Monestir de Pedralbes

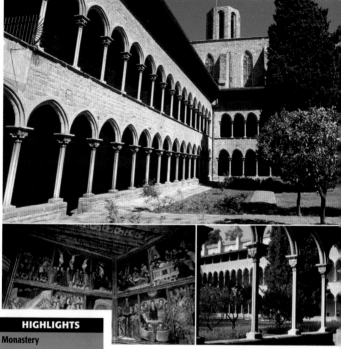

HIGHLIGHTS

Monastery
● Chapel of San Miguel, with 14th-century paintings by Spanish painter and miniaturist Ferrer Bassa
● Tomb of Queen Elisenda, the monastery's founder
● Medieval medicinal garden in the cloister

TIP

● Combine your trip to the museum with a visit to the charming Parc de l'Oreneta, a short walk uphill from the monastery, or a visit to the church next door (open daily 11–1, ☎ 93 203 77 79).

Only a bus ride away from the bustle of central Barcelona stands one of Europe's best-preserved and most atmospheric medieval monasteries. It has an intriguing museum of monastic life.

Monastic museum Once a foothill village outside Barcelona, Pedralbes still exudes a rustic atmosphere, with a cobbled street leading steeply upward to the fortresslike walls of the great monastery. The nuns first came here in the 14th century and their successors still worship in the austere church. They have had a new residence since 1983, and the historic parts of the monastery have become a fascinating museum of monastic life. The building contains numerous works of art, liturgical objects and furniture that the nuns accumulated over the centuries. The

FURTHER AFIELD

★ TOP 25

core of the establishment is the Gothic cloister, three floors high, with elegant columns and capitals. In the middle are palms, orange trees and cypresses; around it are spaces that once housed community activities. The simple cells contrast with the grandeur of the refectory with its vaulted ceiling, and you'll see a pharmacy, infirmary, the kitchens and the great cistern. The chapter house has mementos of monastic life, including the funereal urn of Sobirana de Olzet, the first abbess.

The Church of Pedralbes The nuns still worship in the Gothic church next to the monastery and the sounds of their vespers are often heard in the street outside. A popular place for locals to tie the knot, it is said that if the bride brings the nuns a dozen eggs the day before the ceremony it won't rain on her wedding day.

THE BASICS

✚ C1
✉ Baixada del Monestir 9
☎ 93 256 34 34
🕐 Apr–Sep Tue–Sat 10–7, Sun 10–8; Oct–Mar Tue–Fri and public hols 10–2, Sat–Sun 10–5. Closed 1 Jan, 1 May, Easter Sun, 24 Jun and 25 Dec
🚊 Reina Elisenda
🚌 22, 63, 64, 78
♿ Good
🎟 Moderate, free first Sun of month (combined ticket with Museu d'Història de la Ciutat); also free on Sun after 3pm

Nou Camp

The Nou Camp, home of FC Barcelona, with their distinctive blue and maroon strip

THE BASICS

www.fcbarcelona.com

➕ B2

✉ Aristides Maillol, Entrance 14

☎ 902 189 900

🕐 Jul to mid-Sep daily 9–7.30; Nov–Mar Mon–Sat 10–6.30, Sun and bank holidays 10–2.30; rest of year Mon–Sat 9.30–7, Sun and bank holidays 9.30–2.30

🚇 Collblanc

🚌 15, 54, 113, L12

♿ Fair

💰 Expensive

HIGHLIGHTS

● Tour of the stadium
● Players' tunnel
● Collection of cups and trophies
● Videos of match highlights

TIP

● Buy tickets in advance online (www.fcbarcelona.com/camp-nou/camp-nou-experience) to avoid queues.

FC Barcelona is one of the richest and most successful football clubs in the world. In 2009, its golden year, the club won all six major Spanish and European trophies at stake.

More than a club The club, usually known simply as Barça, has worn the distinctive 'blau-grana' (blue and maroon) striped shirts since its earliest days. The suppression of Catalan language and traditions under the Franco regime made FC Barcelona a potent symbol of Catalan identity, and Barça's slogan remains 'Més que un club' – 'More than a club'. The 99,000-seat Nou Camp stadium is the home of the club, and was originally built in the 1950s thanks in part to its members, who paid their fees early to meet the building costs. Currently the biggest football stadium in Europe, it was set to be expanded to striking designs by Norman Foster, although the plans have been shelved indefinitely owing to the Spanish economic crisis.. If you want to go to a match, especially against arch-rivals Real Madrid, reserve early; most seats will be taken by the club's 170,000 members.

Nou Camp Experience The museum dedicated to FC Barcelona is one of the city's most popular attractions. In the glossy, interactive galleries, you can admire the team's collection of cups and trophies, relive moments of glory in the video displays, and take in a vast collection of memorabilia devoted to the team. A tour of the stadium, including the players' tunnel and dressing rooms, remains the undisputed highlight of the visit.

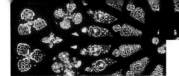

More to See

COSMOCAIXA

www.cosmocaixa.es

Housed in a splendid *modernista* building at the foot of the Tibidabo heights, this Museum of Science is the finest of its kind in Spain. Many of the exhibits and displays encourage participation, and it is loved by children.

➕ G1 ✉ Carrer de Isaac Newton 26 ☎ 93 212 60 50 🕐 Tue–Sun 10–8 🍴 Café 🚇 Tibidabo, then Tramvia Blau ♿ Good 🎫 Moderate

EL FÒRUM

In 2004 the city held a six-month-long 'cultural olympics' in this purpose-built site. The success of the event was debatable, but its legacy, the massive Forum complex, is an asset to Barcelona's outdoor public spaces. It's now mainly used for large-scale music events, but at other times you are free to wander. The stunning cobalt blue Fòrum building is now the Museu Blau, the main seat of the city's Museu de Ciències Naturals, the fun, child-pleasing natural history museum, with plenty of interactive exhibits.

➕ Off map ✉ Rambla Prim 1 🕐 Check www.museublau.bcn.cat for opening times of Museu Blau 🚇 El Maresme/Fòrum

PALAU DE PEDRALBES

The Palau de Pedralbes was donated to the Spanish monarchs by the Güell family in the 1920s, when it was expanded to accommodate its new royal owners. Eusebi Güell, a wealthy industrialist, was Gaudí's most important benefactor, and Gaudí was responsible for the charming fountain in the gardens, as well as the magnificent gates bearing a terrifying wrought-iron dragon, which adorn the gatehouse at the back of the property. The palace is not currently open to the public, but its glorious gardens are perfect for a stroll or a picnic, and provide a charming backdrop for summer concerts held as part of the annual Pedralbes Festival (end-June/early July).

➕ C2 ✉ Diagonal 686 🕐 Daily 10–dusk 🚇 Palau Reial 🚌 7, 33, 67, 74, 75 ♿ Fair 🎫 Access to gardens free

FURTHER AFIELD ★ MORE TO SEE

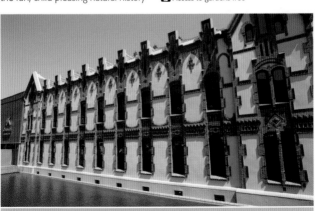

The CosmoCaixa houses Barcelona's Museum of Science

PARC D'ATRACCIONS DE TIBIDABO

www.tibidabo.cat

Built on several levels of the mountain, high-tech attractions sit alongside traditional fairground rides—some features, like the red monoplane (1922) and the Haunted Castle (1955), have entertained for years. El Caní del Cel is a mini version of the park featuring some attractions aimed at younger children and a museum of automation. ➕ Off map ✉ Plaça del Tibidabo ☎ 93 211 79 42 🕐 Opening hours change weekly; check website for times 🚃 FGC Tibidabo then Tramvia Blau and funicular to park 🎟 Tibidabo: expensive; Caní del Cel: moderate

PARC DE COLLSEROLA

www.parcdecollserola.net

Many bring their bikes to this rural park north of the city and ride along the Carretera de les Aigües, a route that skirts the western flank of Tibidabo and offers a spectacular panorama of the entire city. There are lots of well-posted walking tracks where you may spot some of the local wildlife that includes the famous *jabalí* (wild boar). The park contains the Museu Casa Verdaguer, former home of Catalonia's most revered poet. The park's information centre can help you out with maps and advice. ➕ Off map ✉ Information centre: Carretera de Vallvidrera a Sant Cugat ☎ Information centre 93 280 35 52; museum 93 204 78 05 🕐 Information centre daily 9.30–3; museum Sat, Sun and hols 10–2 🍴 Bar/restaurant 🚃 Baixador de Vallvidrera (FGC) then short walk 🎟 Museum: free

TORRE DE COLLSEROLA

This spiky, futuristic landmark high on the hills of Collserola was built as a communications tower for the 1992 Olympic Games. It's the highest point in the city, and visitors can ascend it via an elevator to the mirador. ➕ Off map ✉ Carretera de Vallvidrera al Tibidabo s/n ☎ 93 211 79 42 🕐 Jul–Aug Wed–Sat noon–11; times can vary other months 🚃 Peu de Funicular (FGC) then funicular and bus 11 🎟 Moderate; combined ticket with Tibidabo available

All the fun of the fair at Tibidabo

A view from Tibidabo toward the Torre de Collserola

There's plenty of choice for places to stay in Barcelona, whatever your budget. It's worth checking out the internet before leaving home to catch some seasonal deals.

Where to Stay

Introduction

All accommodation in Catalonia is officially regulated by the Generalitat, the regional government, and is broken down into two main categories, hotels and *hostals*.

What's the Difference?

Hotels are denoted by (H) and rated on a scale of one to five stars. All rooms must have a private bathroom to qualify as a hotel, and the number of stars is determined by the amenities provided. Simpler hotels rarely have restaurants or provide breakfast. In the past five years Barcelona has seen an explosion of smart urban hotels. Facilities such as rooftop pools, stylish lobbies and designer features are becoming more and more common. *Hostals* (HS) sometimes classify themselves as *fondes*, *pensións* or *residències*. They're rated on a scale of one to three stars and are normally less expensive than hotels. Many have been renovated over the past 15 years or so and will have some rooms with bathrooms. *Hostals* tend to be family-run; very few have restaurants and many don't serve breakfast.

Reservations

Despite the plethora of new accommodation, finding a room in Barcelona can be difficult, especially during major trade events, so it pays to book as far ahead as you can to secure something central. If you haven't reserved a room in advance, the tourist offices in the Plaça de Catalunya and the Plaça de Sant Jaume have hotel reservation desks where you will usually be able to find something. They charge a deposit against the cost of the room.

WHERE TO STAY

If you want to be in the heart of the action, reserve accommodation around the Ramblas or in the Barri Gòtic, where there's a huge choice, including budget options. The quieter Eixample, too, is well endowed with hotels, and is generally safer than downtown. Nicest of all are either the classy Ribera, or Gràcia, with its laid-back, intimate atmosphere, though hotels in these areas are scarce.

Budget Hotels

PRICES

Expect to pay between €60 and €90 for a budget hotel

BONIC B&B

www.bonic-barcelona.com
Nothing is too much trouble for the friendly owner of the Bonic B&B, which lives up to its name ('Pretty B&B') with pretty, thoughtfully decorated rooms and a lounge area full of extra details like fresh flowers, newspapers and magazines. Bathrooms are shared, but are always immaculate, and a simple continental breakfast is included in the price.
🕂 G8 ☒ Carrer Josep Anselm Clavé 9 ☎ 62 605 34 34 🔘 Passeig de Gràcia

CASA GRÀCIA

http://casagraciabcn.com
Perfectly located overlooking the swanky Passeig de Gràcia, just steps from La Pedrera and the Casa Batlló, this attractive guest house offers simple, stylish rooms, a huge shared kitchen, a cosy living room with comfy armchairs, and a spacious terrace where you can soak up the sun.
🕂 H6 ☒ Passeig de Gràcia 116 ☎ 93 187 44 97 🔘 Universitat

CHIC & BASIC TALLERS

www.chicandbasic.com
The name says it all for this boutique *hostal*.

Rooms are a bit small, but are decked out in minimalist decor and extras such as flat-screen TVs and iPod docks.
🕂 G7 ☒ Carrer Tallers 82 ☎ 93 302 51 83 🔘 Universitat

EQUITY SEA POINT HOSTEL

www.equity-point.com
A lively beachfront location makes this place hugely popular with young people. Rooms range from 4 to 8 beds and all have private bathrooms. Free WiFi access and breakfast.
🕂 H9 ☒ Plaça del Mar 1-4 ☎ 93 224 70 75 🔘 Barceloneta

HOSTAL GIRONA

www.hostalgirona.com
The reception area, with its antique furniture and Persian rugs, gives a foretaste of the quality of this

SELF-CATERING

Barcelona has hundreds of self-catering holiday apartments available for short-term rent. Unless you are in Barcelona already, the best place to reserve self-catering accommodation is on the internet. Reputable agencies include www.oh-barcelona.com and www.selfcatering-holidays.com. Check out the location from an independent source such as www.tmb.net and ask about extra costs such as cleaning.

superb *hostal*. Rooms are bright and simple, with big windows and tiled floors; some have private bathrooms, and many have balconies overlooking Carrer Girona or the inner courtyard.
🕂 H7 ☒ Carrer de Girona 24 ☎ 93 265 02 59; fax 93 265 85 32 🔘 Urquinaona

HOSTAL ORLEANS

www.hostalorleans.com
Between Barceloneta's beach and the trendy El Born district, you couldn't do much better on a budget. Most rooms have been refurbished and are comfortable with en suites. Some look out onto a busy thoroughfare, so if noise is an issue ask for an interior room.
🕂 H8 ☒ Avinguda Marquès de Argentera 13 ☎ 93 319 73 82 🔘 Barceloneta

HOTEL CURIOUS

www.hotelcurious.com
This renovated, family-run *hostal* is located in the heart of the Raval, close to Las Ramblas. Hardwood floors and chocolate, grape and cream decor, with splashes of photographic wall art, denote tasteful design. Free WiFi and a hearty buffet breakfast are a plus. Rooms are not overly large, but given the location, you probably won't be spending much time inside.
🕂 G7 ☒ Carrer del Carme 25 ☎ 93 301 44 84 🔘 Liceu

Mid-Range Hotels

Expect to pay between
€90 and €150 for a
mid-range hotel

BANYS ORIENTALS
www.hotelbanysorientals.com
Situated on one of the
Born's most bustling
streets, this friendly hotel
lives up to the area's
style credentials without
skimping on the service.
It offers larger suites in an
annexe in a nearby build-
ing. A gem.
⊞ H8 ✉ Carr de Argentería
37 ☎ 93 268 84 60; fax 93
268 84 61 Ⓜ Jaume 1

BARCELÓ RAVAL
www.barceloraval.com
A striking cylindrical building, where the rooms
are spacious and afford
splendid views, boasts a
hip 'James Bond meets
Barbarella' decor, with
70s-inspired furniture and
splashes of bold colour.
The rooftop terrace is not
overly large, but redeemed
by the fact that you can
walk around its entire
diameter and admire the
city's skyline from all 360
degrees. Downstairs the
B-Lounge hosts DJs on the
weekends, which draws a
hip, international crowd.
⊞ F7 ✉ Rambla del Raval
17-21 ☎ 93 320 14 90; fax
93 320 14 94 Ⓜ Drassanes

GAUDÍ
www.hotelgaudi.es
No idle use of the great
architect's name, this

73-room, modern hotel
has an enviable location
opposite the Palau Güell.
⊞ G8 ✉ Carrer Nou de la
Rambla 12 ☎ 93 317 90 32;
fax 93 412 26 36 Ⓜ Liceu

HOTEL 54
www.hotel54barceloneta.com
The ultra-urban Hotel
54 is one of very few
hotels in Barceloneta, so
if staying a stone's throw
from the beach in stylish
surrounds sounds appeal-
ing then look no further.
Rooms are small, but with
all the designer trappings
and fabulous views of the
port from curtain glass
windows. The rooftop
bar and terrace is a great
place to chill out.
⊞ H9 ✉ Passeig de Joan de
Borbo 54 ☎ 93 225 00 54; fax
93 225 00 80 Ⓜ Barceloneta

HOTEL BALMES
www.derbyhotels.com
A small outdoor pool in
a pretty rear garden sets
this great-value, three-star
hotel apart from the rest in
its category, and can prove
a godsend in the hot sum-

RESERVING
ACCOMMODATION

Barcelona is a great magnet
for business visitors, and
reserving early is a must if
you are to have much choice
in where to stay. The past
decade's building boom
boosted the number of
luxury hotels, but also swept
away some of the more
modest accommodation.

mer months. Conveniently
close to the shopping hub
of Passeig de Grácia, the
Balmes' rooms, while not
overly spacious, are stylish
and comfortable and the
hotel also offers a Jacuzzi
and sauna.
⊞ G5 ✉ Carrer Mallorca
216 ☎ 93 451 19 14; fax 93
451 00 49 Ⓜ Diagonal

HOTEL CONSTANZA
www.hotelconstanza.com
Representing great value
for money, this elegant,
Japanese-inspired bou-
tique hotel is brilliantly
situated for shopping and
sights, and has a fabulous
roof terrace where you
can lounge in comfort.
⊞ H6 ✉ Carrer del Bruc 33
☎ 93 270 19 10; fax 93 317
40 24 Ⓜ Urquinaona

HOTEL JAZZ
www.hoteljazz.com
A chic, modern hotel with
an unbeatably central
location on one of the
city's main shopping
streets, this has bright
soundproofed rooms,
a fantastic roof terrace
with a plunge pool and
friendly, helpful staff.
⊞ G7 ✉ Carrer Pelai 3
☎ 93 552 96 96
Ⓜ Catalunya

HOTEL PRAKTIK
www.praktikhotels.com
A 19th-century building
in the Eixample has been
made over to a chilled,
minimalist, urban hotel
while still keeping original
features such as colourful
mosaic flooring and florid

ceiling mouldings. Some rooms have balconies or a private terrace and there is free WiFi.
🞢 H6 ✉ Carrer de Diputació 325 ☎ 93 467 52 79; fax 93 467 31 10 Ⓜ Girona, Tetuan

HOTEL SANT AUGUSTÍ
www.hotelsa.com
This old monastery building on a tree-shaded Raval square was converted to a hotel in 1840, making it the oldest in Barcelona. It's kept up with the times and its handsome, high-ceilinged rooms are now well-equipped and comfortable; two are suitable for disabled guests. The greenery-filled, elegant marble lobby gives access to a relaxing bar and restaurant.
🞢 G7 ✉ Plaça de Sant Agustí 3 ☎ 93 318 16 58; fax 93 317 29 28 Ⓜ Liceu

HOTEL SOHO
www.hotelsohobarcelona.com
This 54-room hotel wears its 'designer' stripes loud and proud, but unlike others in its genre, the mod-con trappings will enhance your stay rather than merely decorate it. There's a stunning terrace with a rooftop plunge pool, where you can cool off after a long day's sightseeing. Ask for a rear room, which are not only quieter but also have a spacious terrace overlooking a courtyard.
🞢 F6 ✉ Gran Via de les Corts Catalanes 543–545

☎ 93 552 96 10; fax 93 552 96 11 Ⓜ Urgell

HUSA ORIENTE
www.husa.es
At the somewhat seedy lower end of the Rambla, the mid-19th-century Oriente has long since ceased to be *the* place to stay in Barcelona, but its ornate public spaces and only slightly less alluring 142 rooms continue to attract customers who like lodgings with some character. Previous guests here include Hans Christian Andersen and Errol Flynn.
🞢 G8 ✉ La Rambla 45 ☎ 93 302 25 58; fax 93 412 38 19 Ⓜ Liceu, Drassanes

MARKET HOTEL
www.markethotel.com.es
Above a smart restaurant of the same name, this hotel offers stylish comfort that is normally associated with much more expensive hotels. Rooms boast hardwood floors, oriental Zen-inspired furniture, quality linen and abstract art. The two self-catering apartments with terraces are unbeatable value. With only 17 rooms (more are being added), you will need to book ahead.

FIRST-TIME VISITORS
The concentration of hotels around the Rambla and within easy walking distance of Plaça de Catalunya makes this area of the city an obvious choice for first-time visitors.

🞢 E7 ✉ Carrer del Comte Borrell 68 ☎ 93 325 12 05; fax 93 424 29 65 Ⓜ Sant Antoni

MUSIK BOUTIQUE HOTEL
www.musikboutiquehotel.com
Tucked away near the magnificent Palau de la Música, this boutique hotel provides chic, modern rooms behind a handsome 18th-century facade. The air-conditioned and soundproofed guest rooms are elegantly decorated and come with extras like iPod docks and WiFi, and some boast private balconies.
🞢 H7 ✉ Carrer Sant Pere Mes Baix 62 ☎ 93 222 55 44 Ⓜ Urquinaona

TURÍN
www.hotelturin.com
This three-star hotel, in a peaceful street, has 59 stylish and functional rooms with balconies. There's a restaurant, conference rooms, a cafeteria and parking, and a roof terrace overlooking the Raval area.
🞢 G7 ✉ Carrer del Pintor Fortuny 9 ☎ 93 302 48 12; fax 93 302 10 05 Ⓜ Catalunya

VILLA EMILIA
www.hotelvillaemilia.com
While not exactly located in the thick of things, this great-value hotel offers tasteful decor and a fabulous rooftop terrace where they serve an evening barbeque in summer.
🞢 E6 ✉ Carrer Calabria 115–117 ☎ 93 252 52 85; fax 93 252 52 86 Ⓜ Rocafort

Luxury Hotels

WHERE TO STAY LUXURY HOTELS

ARTS BARCELONA
www.hotelartsbarcelona.com
483 up-to-the-minute luxury rooms overlooking Port Olímpic and private suites with butler service in a glass skyscraper.
 J9 ✉ Carrer de la Marina 19–21 ☎ 93 221 10 00; fax 93 221 10 70 Ⓜ Ciutadella–Vila Olímpica

CASA FUSTER
www.barcelonacasafuster hotel.com
Designed in 1911, this magnificent building has undergone a restoration that unites sleek modern design with the glory of the past. The opulent rooms retain period features but offer cutting-edge technology and superb comfort. The ground-floor Café Vienés is a superb tribute to the past.
G5 ✉ Passeig de Gràcia 132 ☎ 93 255 30 00; fax 93 255 30 02 Ⓜ Diagonal

GRAND HOTEL CENTRAL
www.grandhotelcentral.com
With the reputation of having the best rooftop terrace in the city, this smooth-as-silk hotel is a popular choice with style setters. Rooms are spacious and emit a sense of refined ambience in calming earth tones.
H7 ✉ Via Laietana 30 ☎ 93 295 79 00; fax 93 268 12 15 Ⓜ Jaume I

HOTEL 1898
www.hotel1898.com
One of the city's most exciting new hotels. An art deco theme prevails, with palms, patterned floors and ship's-cabin style in the 169 rooms. Spa and rooftop pool; it's the only luxury option right on Las Ramblas.
G7 ✉ Las Ramblas 109 ☎ 93 552 95 52; fax 93 552 95 50 Ⓜ Catalunya

HOTEL DUQUESA DE CARDONA
www.hduquesadecardona.com
A romantic hotel in a stunning spot occupying a restored 16th-century building, which has been fitted with natural materials that focus on its air of understated luxury. Roof terrace with swimming pool and a restaurant serving modern Catalan food.

G8 ✉ Passeig de Colom 12 ☎ 93 268 90 90; fax 93 268 29 31 Ⓜ Drassanes

HOTEL NERI
www.hotelneri.com
A handsome palace deep in the Gothic quarter stunningly made over into a luxurious boutique hotel. Sumptuous, orientalist interiors combined with mod cons and smooth comfort.
G7 ✉ Carrer Sant Sever 5 ☎ 93 304 06 55; fax 93 304 03 37 Ⓜ Jaume 1

HOTEL PULITZER
www.hotelpulitzer.es
The Pullitzer stands just behind the Plaça Catalunya, providing stylish hotel comfort in the city's main hub. The rooms and public areas contain an impressive collection of antiques and abstract art, and the Japanese-style bathrooms and rooftop terrace are a real draw.
G7 ✉ Carrer Bergara 8 ☎ 93 481 67 67; fax 93 481 64 64 Ⓜ Catalunya

W BARCELONA
www.starwoodhotels.com
Jutting out from the southernmost tip of Barceloneta beach, the soaring, sail-shaped W Barcelona is placed to impress. Glorious coastal views encase the spacious rooms while a top floor bar and mezzanine-level wet deck provide a resort-type experience.
Off map ✉ Plaça de la Rosa dels Vents 1 ☎ 93 295 28 00; fax 93 181 50 00 🚌 64

Use this section to familiarize yourself
with travel to and within Barcelona.
The Essential Facts will give you insider
knowledge of the city. You'll also find a
few basic language tips.

Planning Ahead

When to Go

Barcelona has no off-season—there is always something to see and do. However, May to June and mid-September to mid-November are ideal visiting times, with perfect temperatures and bearable crowds. Summer can be very hot, and you'll have to contend with huge crowds.

TIME

Spain is 6 hours ahead of New York City, 9 hours ahead of Los Angeles, and 1 hour ahead of the UK.

AVERAGE DAILY MAXIMUM TEMPERATURES

JAN	FEB	MAR	APR	MAY	JUN	JUL	AUG	SEP	OCT	NOV	DEC
57°F	59°F	63°F	66°F	72°F	77°F	84°F	84°F	81°F	73°F	64°F	59°F
14°C	15°C	17°C	19°C	22°C	25°C	29°C	29°C	27°C	23°C	18°C	15°C

Spring (March to May) is a good time to visit; pleasantly warm, though it can be cloudy.
Summer (June to September) is the hottest season with very high temperatures in July and August.
Autumn (October to November) is normally Barcelona's wettest season, with heavy rain and thunderstorms as summer heat abates.
Winter (December to February) brings rain up to Christmas, followed by cooler, drier weather, though temperatures are rarely much below 10°C (50°F).

WHAT'S ON

January *Three Kings* (6 Jan): The kings arrive by boat and shower children with sweets.
February/March *Carnival:* Boisterous pre-Lenten celebrations include a major costumed procession and the symbolic burial of a sardine. Sitges *Carnival* is particularly festive.
Easter Celebrated in style in the outer districts with a southern Spanish population.
April *St. Jordi (St.George's Day*, 23 Apr): The festival of Catalonia's patron saint is marked by lovers' gifts: roses for the woman, a book for the man. There are open-air book fairs and impressive floral displays.
June/July *Sant Joan* (23–24 Jun): An excuse for mass partying and for locals to set off fireworks from their balconies or down on the beach.
Festival del Grec (Jun–Aug): A festival of music, plays and dance.
August *Festa Major de Gràcia:* A week of street celebrations in the city's most vibrant suburb, village-like Gràcia.
September *Diada de Catalunya* (11 Sep): Flags wave on the Catalan National Day, and political demonstrations are likely.
Festas de la Mercè (19–25 Sep): The four-day festival celebrating the city's patron saint, Our Lady of Mercy, is Barcelona's biggest. Music, plays, *sardana* dancing, parades, fireworks and spectacles featuring giants, dragons and *castellers* (human towers) all occur.
December *The Christmas Season:* Preparations include a grand crib in Plaça de Sant Jaume (▷ 51) and a market in front of the cathedral.

Useful Websites

www.barcelonaturisme.com
Barcelona's official tourist website has a wealth of information on every aspect of the city. In English, and regularly updated, it's the obvious place to research your trip. You can buy tickets to most sights and attractions online.

www.spain.info
The main Spanish tourist board site is loaded with details about both Barcelona and its local environs.

www.barcelona-metropolitan.com
The city's premier English-language magazine gives the low-down on what's on and what's new in the bar, restaurant and nightclub scene, as well as inspiration for days out of town and a handy classified section for apartments and jobs.

www.barcelonahotels.es
Run by Barcelona's hotelier association, this site has a good choice of mid-range, mid-price hotels with online booking.

www.bcn.cat
This site, in English, is run by Barcelona's city council and is primarily aimed at locals. There is an excellent tourism section, with details of opening times, exhibitions and more.

www.tmb.net
All you need to know about fares, routes and the timetables of Barcelona's bus and metro systems.

www.fcbarcelona.com
Even if you're not a football fan, this official site gives an insight into the passions the team evokes.

www.lecool.com
A carefully selected roundup of hip cultural and music events for the coming week.

PRIME TRAVEL SITES

www.fodors.com
A complete travel-planning site. You can research prices and weather; book air tickets, cars and rooms; ask questions (and get answers) from fellow travellers; and find links to other sites.

www.renfe.com
The official site of Spanish National Railways.

www.wunderground.com
Good weather forecasting, updated three times daily.

INTERNET CONNECTION

Barcelona is one of the easiest European cities in which to go online. More and more hotels are offering WiFi options as are many bars and cafés (look for the 'WiFi' symbol). *Locutorios* are cheap call venues, with phone booths installed that let you call home at a less expensive rate than either the hotels or public phone booths. A huge percentage of these also have internet facilities and most are in the Raval, Barri Gòtic and Barceloneta districts. Free 'hotspots' in the city include Sants train station and Santa Caterina market— though connection is limited to an hour. See www.bcn.cat/barcelonawifi/en for a full list of hotspots.

Getting There

FARMACIA

INSURANCE

US citizens should check their insurance coverage and buy a supplementary policy as needed. EU nationals receive medical treatment on production of the European emergency health card (EHIC), an electronic card that replaced the old E–111. You should obtain this before leaving home. Full health and travel insurance is still advised. In case of emergency go to the casualty department of any of the major hospitals; Clínic (Villaroel 170, tel 93 227 54 00, 🚇 Hospital Clínic) and Perecamps (Avda Drassanes 13–15, tel 93 441 06 00, 🚇 Drassanes) are the two most central.

BARCELONA AIRPORT

Barcelona airport consists of two terminals; T1 and T2. Over 50 companies operate from T1, including Star Alliance, British Airways, Iberia and the low-cost Spanish carrier Vueling. More airlines are being added, so check which terminal your flight leaves from. A bus shuttle runs between TI and T2 and the airport's train station (at T2); the journey takes 10 minutes. Both terminals have tourist information desks, currency exchanges, shops and other facilities.

AIRPORTS

Barcelona's modern airport is spread over two terminals at El Prat de Llobregat. T1 services most international carriers, while T2 services smaller companies. Connections to both are good, though vary from one to the other; make sure you know which terminal you need before setting off.

FROM BARCELONA AIRPORT (EL PRAT)

Barcelona's airport (☎ 902 40 47 04; www.aena.es) is well served by city links. The convenient Aerobus service connects both T1 and T2 with Plaça de Catalunya via Plaça d'Espanya and Gran Via de les Corts Catalanes (and Sants station for travel to the airport). The service operates every 8–12 minutes in both directions, from 6am to 1am. Allow 30 minutes for T2 (€4.25) and 40 minutes for T1 (€5); check which terminal the bus goes to before boarding.

Trains (line 10) link the airport with Sants Estació de França. They run every 30 minutes, from 5.20am to 10.42pm, and cost around €2.50 one-way. The journey takes 33 minutes. Taxis are available outside the airport terminals; the journey takes about 20–30 minutes, depending on traffic, and costs about €25 from T2 and €30 from T1.

ARRIVING BY TRAIN

Barcelona is connected to all major cities within Spain and a number of destinations in Europe, namely Paris, Geneva, Zürich and Milan. These

trains arrive and depart at Sants Estació, the city's main station, which also has regular bus and metro services to central Barcelona and elsewhere. A few regional trains leave from the stations Estació de França in the old town (predominantly southbound) and from Passeig de Gràcia in the new town (mainly northbound).

ARRIVING BY BUS
Direct bus services operate from several European countries. The bus station is Estació d'Autobus Barcelona Nord, next to Arc de Triomf rail and metro station ☎ 902 26 06 06; www.barcelonanord.com.

ARRIVING BY CAR
Barcelona is connected by the AP7 toll *autopista* to the French frontier and motorway network at La Jonquera (144km/90 miles northeast). Toulouse is 368km (245 miles) north via N152, the French frontier at Puigcerdà and RN20. Motorway access to the rest of Spain is via *autopista* AP2 and AP7. However, driving is not recommended in Barcelona itself; traffic is heavy and can be intimidating, most of the city streets are part of what can be a bewildering one-way system, and parking is at a premium, with virtually no on-street parking for visitors in the downtown area. If you are driving, you could leave your car in one of the long-term airport parking areas.

ARRIVING BY SEA
Car ferry services from Britain to Spain are operated by Brittany Ferries (☎ 0871 244 0744, Plymouth–Santander, Portsmouth–Santander and Portsmouth–Bilbao). Ferries and cruise ships arrive at Barcelona's Port Terminal at the southern end of Las Ramblas. Ferries connect Rome and Genova in Italy and the Balearic Islands of Ibiza, Mallorca and Menorca. For the latter, the largest operator is Trasmediterránea ☎ 902 45 46 45; www.tras-mediterranea.es.

Getting Around

MAPS

If you want additional maps, the tourist offices provide a fairly comprehensive free street map and also sell more detailed ones at a cost of €1.50. Metro maps (ask for *una guia del metro*) are available at all metro stations, and you can pick up bus maps, which help you to make full use of the integrated TMB, city transport authority, at their main information office at metro Universitat.

VISITORS WITH DISABILITIES

Barcelona's public transport system has improved greatly for visitors with disabilities. All buses have ramps for wheelchair access and many Metro stations are being adapted with elevators. For information see www.tmb. net or look for the disabled symbol on the metro maps. The Taxi Amic service (☎ 93 420 80 88) has wheelchair-adapted taxis; call well in advance to book. New buildings and museums have excellent facilities for visitors with disabilities, though some older attractions have yet to be converted. Check out www.accessiblebarcelona. com for lots of information on the city's wheelchair-enabled facilities (including hotels) and organized tours.

Although Barcelona is a walker's city *par excellence*, at some point you will need to use the first-rate bus and metro (subway) system, which is supplemented by funiculars, a new, if limited, tramline and the historic Tramvia Blau, which climbs to the base of Tibidabo. Buses, the metro and the suburban railway, FGC, are fully integrated and tickets can be used on any of them for either one-system or combined journeys. Pick up a map of the network from a tourist information area or one of the TMB offices; these are in the metro stations at Plaça de la Universitat, Barcelona-Sants and Sagrada Família and Sagrera.

● Information line ☎ 902 07 50 27

TICKETS

One-way tickets are available, but it makes sense to pay for multiple journeys using one of several types of *targeta* (travelcard):

● *Targeta* 10 (or T-10) valid for 10 trips by metro (and FGC) or bus.

● *Targeta* T-Mes is valid for unlimited trips within 30 days by metro (and FGC) or bus.

● You must cancel one unit of a *targeta* per journey undertaken by inserting it into the automatic machine at the entry to a station or aboard a bus. Changing from metro (or FGC) to bus or vice versa within 1 hour counts as one trip.

● *Targetas* are available only from metro stations; most are operated by vending machine.

METRO

There are 11 metro lines now, identified by number and colour. Direction is indicated by the name of the station at the end of the line.

● The network covers most parts of the city and is being extended Ⓜ Mon–Thu and Sun 5am–midnight, Fri and the evening before a public holiday 5am–2am, Sat 24 hours.

TRAINS

● Many mainline trains run beneath the city stopping at the underground stations at Passeig

de Gràcia and Plaça de Catalunya.
● Rail information: National ☎ 902 240 202

BUSES

Buses run 6.30am–10pm, though routes vary.
A free map detailing all bus services is available
from TMB's information points. As well as one-
way tickets, several types of *targeta* (travelcard)
can be used on the metro and buses.
● *Targetas* can be bought only at metro
stations, not onboard buses.
● More information (including frequency of
service) is given on the panels at bus stops.
● There is a night service, the *Nitbus*, with
routes around Plaça de Catalunya.
● Useful tourist routes include numbers 22
(Plaça de Catalunya–Gràcia–Tramvia Blau–
Pedralbes Monastery) and 24 (Plaça de
Catalunya–Gràcia–Parc Güell).

TAXIS

● Black-and-yellow taxis can easily be hailed
on the street when displaying a green light
and the sign Lliure/Libre (free). There are large
taxi stands at the northern end of Las Ramblas
(opposite Plaça Catalunya) and at the southern
end opposite the Columbus monument.
● Fares are not expensive, but a series of
supplements—for luggage, airport runs and
past-midnight rides—can bump up the fare.

ORGANIZED SIGHTSEEING

The best buy in city sightseeing is the Bus
Turístic, which has three routes—one running
north of the city (green), one south and west
(red) and one eastward (blue). One- and two-
day tickets entitle you to discounts on many
sights. Tickets are sold at the Tourist Information
Centre in Plaça Catalunya and TMB offices at
Sants, Universitat, Sagrera and Sagrada Família
metro stations. Barcelona City Tour (☎ 93 317
64 54) offers the same service from a red
double-decker bus. Various other organizations
provide individual guides, who can give you a
more personal introduction to Barcelona.

TAXI CONTACTS

If you need to call a taxi, try
these reputable services:
Barna Taxi
✉ 93 357 77 55
Servi Taxi
✉ 93 330 03 00
Radio Taxi
✉ 902 222 111
Taxi Class Rent
✉ 93 307 07 07

TOURIST INFORMATION

➕ G7 ✉ Plaça Catalunya
s/n 🕐 Daily 9–9

➕ D5 ✉ Estació de Sants
🕐 Mon–Fri 8–8, Sat–Sun
8–2 (until 8 in summer)

➕ G8 ✉ Carrer Ciutat 2
(Ajuntament) 🕐 Mon–Fri
9–8, Sat 10–8, Sun 10–2

➕ G7 ✉ Las Ramblas 115
🕐 Daily 9–9

➕ G7 ✉ La Rambla 115
🕐 Daily 9–9

➕ Off map ✉ El Prat
airport terminals T1 and T2
🕐 Daily 9–9

Tourist Info phone line:
☎ 93 285 38 34

Essential Facts

TRAVELLER BEWARE

Be aware that, in certain areas of the city, petty crime rates are very high. Often thefts will occur using diversionary tactics to distract tourists' attention. The Raval area is particularly notorious after dark. Follow common-sense rules, such as carrying little cash and few credit cards, don't wear expensive jewellery, and leave passports and tickets in the hotel. If you are unfortunate enough to be a victim, you must report the theft to the police and be issued with the crime report in order to claim on your insurance.

USEFUL PHONE NUMBERS

● Police, fire and ambulance ☎ 112
● Nacional Police ☎ 091
● Local police ☎ 092
● General city information ☎ 010
● To report a crime ☎ 902 102 112 (English-speaking operators 9am–9pm)

CUSTOMS REGULATIONS

● The limits for non-EU visitors are 200 cigarettes or 50 cigars, or 250g of tobacco; 1 litre of spirits (over 22 per cent) or 2 litres of fortified wine, 2 litres of still wine; 50g of perfume. The guidelines for EU residents (for personal use) are 800 cigarettes, or 200 cigars, or 1kg tobacco; 10 litres of spirits (over 22 per cent), 20 litres of aperitifs, or 90 litres of wine, of which 60 can be sparkling, or 110 litres of beer.
● Visitors under 17 are not entitled to the tobacco and alcohol allowances.

ELECTRICITY

● The standard current is 220/225 volts AC (sometimes 110/125 volts AC).
● Plugs are of round two-pin type. US visitors require an adaptor and a transformer.

OPENING HOURS

● Banks: Mon–Fri 8.30–2.
● Shops: Mon–Sat 9 or 10–1.30, 4.30–8 (hours vary). Larger shops/department stores may open all day. Some Sunday opening.
● Some small museums shut for lunch, close early on Sunday and are shut all day Monday.
● Pharmacies (*Farmàcies*) offer a wider range of treatments and medicines than in many countries. Opening hours: Mon–Sat 9–1.30, 4.30–8 (some close on Saturday afternoons).

HEALTH

● If you need a doctor, ask at your hotel as a first step. If you do not have private insurance you will only be entitled to see a doctor working within the Spanish State Health Service.
● Pharmacies are marked by a flashing green cross and operate a rota system so there is at least one open in every neighbourhood 24 hours a day. Farmàcia Alvarez, Passeig de Gràcia 26 and Farmàcia Clapés, La Rambla 98 are always open 24/7.

FARMACIA

MONEY
● Credit cards are widely accepted and can be used in hotels, restaurants and shops. You will be asked to produce photo identification such as a passport or EU driving licence when using a credit card. Credit cards can also be used in automatic ticketing machines for the metro and RENFE (Spanish rail) lines.
● ATMs (*cajeros*) are found all over the city, with operating instructions in several languages, including English.
● Many money transfers and exchange offices such as Western Union can be found along Las Ramblas.

TOURIST CARDS AND SERVICES
Various *targetas* (cards) for tourists are available at the Tourist Information Offices (▷ 119) offering great discounts on the main sites and more.
● The Barcelona Card (cost €37–€62, valid for 2, 3, 4, 5 or 6 days) gives unlimited access to public transport and discounts at over 100 museums, monuments, restaurants and shops.
● The Articket allows entry to the city's major museums and galleries; cost €22.
● Barcelona Turisme's walking tours are organized around themes, and offer great value as they always include at least one trip to a museum; cost approx €11–€21.
● Barcelona Turisme is not the only place where tourists can gather information. The Centre d'Informació de la Virreina (✉ Las Ramblas 99 ☎ 93 301 7775) has brochures and information on the city's fiestas and cultural events, while the Palau Robert (✉ Passeig de Gràcia 107 ☎ 93 238 4000) has information on out-of-town destinations within Catalonia.

EUROS
The euro is the official currency of Spain. Notes come in denominations of 5, 10, 20, 50, 100, 200 and 500 euros and coins in denominations of 1, 2, 5, 10, 20 and 50 cents, and 1 and 2 euros.

10 euros

50 euros

200 euros

500 euros

ETIQUETTE
● It's normal to wish people *bon dia*. Friends exchange kisses on both cheeks.
● Expect to find unabashed smokers in public places.
● Do not wear shorts or short skirts in churches.

CONSULATES
Canada	✉ Plaça de Catalunya 9	☎ 93 270 36 14
Ireland	✉ Gran Via Carles III 94	☎ 93 491 50 21
United Kingdom	✉ Diagonal 477	☎ 90 210 95 36
United States	✉ Passeig Reina Elisenda 23	☎ 93 280 22 27

FARMACIA

CHILDREN

● Children are welcome everywhere, but the standard and range of child-specific facilities do not match those available in the UK or US.
● Mother and baby-changing and feeding facilities are rare.
● Hotels will generally be happy to put an extra bed and/or cot in your room for an additional charge.
● Public transport is free for children under 4, but access to the metro with pushchairs (strollers) can be difficult.
● There are no menus specifically for kids, but most restaurants will happily serve children's portions.
● You will find children's play areas in parks and squares all over the city.
● Barcelona's beaches are clean, with play areas, showers and kiosks.
● The tourist board keeps a list of child-minding services.
● You can hire a stroller from Baby Travelling (babytravelling.com).

TELEPHONES

● New public phones accept coins, phonecards and credit cards. Phonecards are available from paper shops and newsstands.
● National operator ☎ 1009.
● International operator: Spain ☎ 1409; elsewhere ☎ 1408.
● Directory Enquiries: 11822; International 11825.
● You must dial Barcelona's code (93), even within Barcelona.
● To phone the US from Spain, prefix the code and number with 001.
● To phone the UK from Spain, dial 00 44, then drop the first zero from the area code.

POST OFFICES

● Main post office (Correu Central) ✉ Plaça Antoni López ☎ 93 486 80 50 🕐 Mon–Fri 8.30–9.30, Sat 8.30–2 🚇 Barceloneta
● Other post offices are at Aragó 282, Ronda Universitat 23 and Carrer València 231.
● Stamps are sold at paper shops and tobacconists.
● Mailboxes are yellow.

NEWSPAPERS

● International papers are sold at newsstands on the Rambla and Passeig de Gràcia.
● The English-language monthly *Barcelona Metropolitan*, launched in 1996, has some listings and is free.
● The main current events periodical is the weekly *Guía del Ocio*.
● *Time Out* in Catalan is also sold.
● The Friday edition of *La Vanguardia* contains a supplement *Què Fem?* which is full of listings.

Language

Catalan now enjoys equal status to Castillian Spanish in Barcelona and Catalonia, and must not be thought of as a dialect. Street signs and official communications are now exclusively in Catalan, but virtually everyone understands Castillian Spanish. Most people in the tourist industry speak some English and French. Any effort to speak Spanish or (especially) Catalan will be welcomed.

SOME SPANISH WORDS TO LOOK OUT FOR:

Spanish/Catalan

buenos días/bon dia	good morning
buenas tardes/ bona tarda	good evening
buenas noches/ bona nit	good night
hola/hola	hello
adiós/adéu	goodbye
gracias/gràcies	thank you
perdóne/perdoni	excuse me
de nada/de res	you're welcome
por favor/si us plau	please
si, no/sí, no	yes, no
abierto/obert	open
cerrado/tancat	closed
iglesia/església	church
palacio/palau	palace
museo/museu	museum
calle/carrer	street
aseos, servicios/ lavabo	restroom, toilet
lunes/dilluns	Monday
martes/dimarts	Tuesday
miércoles/dimecres	Wednesday
jueves/dijous	Thursday
viernes/divendres	Friday
sábado/dissabte	Saturday
domingo/diumenge	Sunday

CALLE OR CARRER

Barcelona's bi-lingualism needs to be understood when getting around. Both the Spanish *Calle* and Catalan *Carrer* are used to mean 'street' though this is mainly dropped in everyday conversation, thus Carrer or Calle de Pau Claris simply becomes 'Pau Claris'. Although by law all nomenclature must be in Catalan, people still use Spanish versions; compare Comerç (Catalan) to Comercio (Spanish) though this rarely causes more than a moment of confusion.

NUMBERS

Spanish/Catalan

un, dos/ uno/una, dos	1, 2
tres, cuatro/ tres, quatre	3, 4
cinco, seis/ cinc, sis	5, 6
siete, ocho/ set, vuit	7, 8
nueve, diez/ nou, deu	9, 10

Timeline

BEFORE 1000

Barcelona's origins date back to 27BC–AD14, when the Romans founded Barcino during the reign of Emperor Augustus.

City walls were built in the late 3rd/early 4th century, as a result of attacks by Franks and Alemanni.

AD415 saw a Visigothic invasion and the establishment of the Kingdom of Tolosa, predecessor of Catalonia. Arabs invaded in 717 and the city became Barjelunah. In 876 the Franks gained control. Catalonia became independent in 988 after the Franks declined to send support against the Moors.

FOR EIXAMPLE

In 1859, officials approved a plan for the Eixample, the grandiose extension of Barcelona beyond the city walls. The plan was finally developed in the late 19th and early 20th century, with many *modernista* buildings.

1131–62 Ramon Berenguer IV reigns and the union of Catalonia and Aragon takes place. Barcelona becomes a major trading city.

1213–76 Jaume I reigns, and conquers Valencia, Ibiza and Mallorca from the Moors. New city walls are built.

1354 The legislative council of Catalonia sets up the Generalitat to control city finances.

1410 Martí I, the last ruler of the House of Barcelona, dies without an heir. Catalonia is now ruled from Madrid, which becomes more interested in transatlantic ventures than the trade of the Mediterranean.

1462–73 The Catalan civil war rages and the economy deteriorates.

1640 Els Segadors (the Reapers) revolt against Castilian rule.

1714 Barcelona is defeated by French and Spanish troops in the War of the Spanish Succession. Catalonia made Spanish province.

1813 Napoleonic troops depart. Textile manufacturing leads to a growth in the city's industry and population.

1888 The Universal Exhibition attracts 2 million visitors.

1909 Barcelona's churches and convents

PHILIP. V.

are set aflame during the Setmana Tràgica (Tragic Week).

1914–18 Barcelona's economy is boosted by Spanish neutrality in World War I.

1931 The Catalan Republic is declared after the exile of King Alfonso XIII.

1939 Barcelona falls to the Nationalists, led by General Franco. Spain remains neutral during World War II.

1975 Franco dies. Restoration of the monarchy under Juan Carlos I allows the re-establishment of the Generalitat as the parliament of an autonomous regional government of Catalonia.

1992 Barcelona hosts the Olympic Games.

2004 Barcelona hosts the UNESCO Universal Forum of Cultures.

2007 The Spanish Government recognizes Catalonia as a 'nation' in the constitution.

2008 The AVE, a high-speed rail network connecting Barcelona and Madrid, comes into service.

2009 Barcelona airport's new terminal opens with capacity for 55 million passengers per year.

2010 Pope Benedict XVI consecrates the Sagrada Família.

FRANCO

In 1936, armed workers in Barcelona defeated an army uprising led by Nationalist General Franco. But resistance to Franco was weakened by internal strife between Communists and Anarchists. In 1939, Barcelona fell to the Nationalists. Catalan identity and culture were crushed during the subsequent Franco dictatorship. The Catalan language was banned and the region suffered economic decline. Franco died in 1975 and the monarchy was restored.

From left: A statue of St. George at the Generalitat; Philip V of Spain; the Monument à Colom; an old Barcelonan street; modernista *buildings in the Ramblas; General Franco*

Index

INDEX

127

Barcelona 25 Best

WRITTEN BY Michael Ivory
ADDITIONAL WRITING Sally Roy
UPDATED BY Mary-Ann Gallagher
SERIES EDITOR Clare Ashton
COVER DESIGN Chie Ushio, Yuko Inagaki
DESIGN WORK Tracey Butler
IMAGE RETOUCHING AND REPRO Ian Little

Published in the United Kingdom by AA Publishing

ISBN 978-0-8041-4328-8

SEVENTH EDITION

SPECIAL SALES
This book is available for special discounts for bulk purchases for sales promotions or premiums. For more information, email specialmarkets@randomhouse.com.

Color separation by AA Digital Department
Printed and bound by Leo Paper Products, China

10 9 8 7 6 5 4 3 2 1

A05132
Maps in this title produced from mapping © MAIRDUMONT / Falk Verlag 2013
Transport map © Communicarta Ltd, UK

The Automobile Association would like to thank the following photographers, companies and picture libraries for their assistance in the preparation of this book.

1 AA/S Day; 2 AA/M Jourdan; 3 AA/M Jourdan; 4t AA/M Jourdan; 4l AA/S Day; 5t AA/M Jourdan; 5 AA/S Day; 6t AA/M Jourdan; 6cl AA/M Jourdan; 6c AA/M Chaplow; 6cr AA/S Day; 6bl AA/M Chaplow; 6bc AA/S Day; 6br AA/M Chaplow; 7t AA/M Jourdan; 7cl AA/S Day; 7c AA/S Day; 7cr AA/M Jourdan; 7bl AA/M Chaplow; 7bc AA/M Chaplow; 7br AA/S Day; 8t AA/M Jourdan; 9t AA/M Jourdan; 10t AA/M Jourdan; 10tr AA/S McBride; 10ctr AA/S McBride; 10cbr AA/S McBride; 10br AA/M Chaplow; 11t AA/M Jourdan; 11tl AA/S McBride; 11ctl AA/S McBride; 11cbl AA/S McBride; 11bl AA/S McBride; 12t AA/M Jourdan; 12bl AA/M Chaplow; 13t AA/M Jourdan; 13tl AA/M Jourdan; 13ctl AA/S McBride; 13cl Digital Vision; 13cbl Photodisc; 13bl Brand X Pics; 14t AA/M Jourdan; 14tr AA/S McBride; 14ctr AA/S McBride; 14cbr AA/S McBride; 14br AA/S McBride; 15t AA/M Jourdan; 15br AA/S McBride; 16t AA/M Jourdan; 16tr AA/S McBride; 16cr AA/S McBride; 16br AA/S Day; 17t AA/M Jourdan; 17tl AA/S Day; 17ctl AA/S Day; 17cbl AA/M Chaplow; 17bl AA/S McBride; 18t AA/M Jourdan; 18tr AA/S Day; 18ctr AA/M Chaplow; 18cbr AA/S Day; 18br AA/M Jourdan; 19t AA/S Day; 19ct AA/M Jourdan; 19c AA/M Jourdan; 19cb AA/M Jourdan; 19b AA/M Chaplow; 20/1 AA/M Chaplow; 24/5 AA/M Jourdan; 25tr AA/M Jourdan; 25cr AA/P Wilson; 26/7 AA/S Day, © 2011 Calder Foundation, New York / DACS London; 27 AA/P Wilson, © Succession Miro/ADAGP, Paris and DACS, London 2011; 28 AA/M Chaplow; 28/9 AA/M Jourdan; 30l AA/S Day; 30r AA/S Day; 31l AA/M Jourdan; 31c AA/M Jourdan; 31r AA/M Jourdan; 32t AA/S Day; 32b AA/M Jourdan; 33 AA/M Bonnet; 34t AA/S Day; 34bl AA/M Jourdan; 34br AA/P Wilson; 35t AA/C Sawyer; 36t AA/S McBride; 37t Digital Vision; 36c AA/M Jourdan; 38t AA/S McBride; 39 AA/S Day; 42l AA/S Day; 42/3t AA/S Day; 42/3c AA/S Day; 43tr AA/M Jourdan; 43cr AA/M Jourdan; 44 AA/M Jourdan; 44/5 AA/S Day; 46 AA/M Jourdan; 46/7t AA/M Chaplow; 46/7c AA/S Day; 47 AA/M Jourdan; 48l AA/M Bonnet; 48c AA/M Bonnet; 48r AA/S Day; 48l AA/S Day; 48c AA/P Wilson; 48r AA/M Chaplow; 49l AA/S McBride; 49r AA/S McBride; 50t AA/S Day; 50bl AA/P Wilson; 50br AA/P Wilson; 51t AA/S Day; 51b AA/S Day; 52 AA/S McBride; 53t AA/S McBride; 54t AA/M Chaplow; 55t Digital Vision; 56 AA/M Jourdan; 57t AA/S McBride; 58t AA/S McBride; 59 Ricard Pla and Pere Vivas/Palau de la Música Catalana; 62l AA/M Jourdan; 62r AA/M Jourdan; 63l AA/M Jourdan; 63c AA/M Chaplow; 63r Las Meninas, No. 30 (1957), Pablo Picasso, Pablo/Museu Picasso, Barcelona, Spain, Giraudon/The Bridgeman Art Library, © Succession Picasso/DACS, London 2011; 64l AA/M Jourdan; 64r Ricard Pla and Pere Vivas/Palau de la Música Catalana; 65l AA/M Chaplow; 65c AA/M Jourdan; 65r AA/M Jourdan; 66l AA/S Day; 66r AA/P Wilson; 67l AA/M Chaplow; 67r AA/M Chaplow; 68l AA/M Jourdan; 68/9t AA/S Day; 68cr AA/M Jourdan; 69cl AA/M Jourdan; 69r AA/M Jourdan; 70l AA/M Jourdan; 70/1 AA/P Wilson; 71 AA/S Day; 72t AA/S Day; 72bl AA/M Jourdan; 72br AA/M Jourdan; 73 AA/C Sawyer; 74t AA/S McBride; 75t AA/S McBride; 76t Photodisc; 77t AA/C Sawyer; 78t AA/S McBride; 78br AA/C Sawyer; 79 AA/S Day; 82 AA/S Day; 82/3 AA/S Day; 83t AA/M Chaplow; 83cl AA/S Day; 83cr AA/M Jourdan; 84 AA/M Bonnet; 85l AA/M Jourdan; 85r AA/M Chaplow; 86l AA/P Wilson; 86/7 AA/S Day; 86cr AA/S Day; 87r AA/M Jourdan; 87c AA/M Chaplow; 88 AA/S Day; 88/9t AA/M Jourdan; 88/9c AA/S Day; 89 AA/M Jourdan; 90 AA/S Day; 90/1 AA/M Jourdan; 91 AA/S Day; 92t AA/S Day; 92bl AA/M Jourdan; 92br AA/M Chaplow; 93t AA/C Sawyer; 93r AA/M Chaplow; 94t AA/M Chaplow; 95t AA/S McBride; 96t Digital Vision; 97t AA/S McBride; 98t AA/C Sawyer; 99 AA/S Day; 102/3t AA/M Jourdan; 102cl AA/M Jourdan; 102/3c AA/S Day; 103 AA/M Jourdan; 104l AA/M Bonnet; 104r AA/M Bonnet; 105t AA/S Day; 105b AA/M Bonnet; 106t AA/S Day; 106bl LH Images/Alamy; 106br AA/S Day; 107 AA/S McBride; 108t AA/C Sawyer; 108tr AA/S McBride; 108ctr AA/S McBride; 108cbr AA/C Sawyer; 108br AA/M Chaplow; 109t AA/C Sawyer; 110t AA/C Sawyer; 111t AA/C Sawyer; 112t AA/C Sawyer; 113 AA/S Day; 114t AA/S McBride; 115t AA/S McBride; 116t AA/S McBride; 117t AA/S McBride; 118t AA/S McBride; 119t AA/S McBride; 120t AA/S McBride; 120l AA/M Jourdan; 121t AA/S McBride; 122t AA/S McBride; 122t AA/M Jourdan; 122/3t AA/M Chaplow; 123t AA/S McBride; 124t AA/S McBride; 124bl AA/P Wilson; 124bc AA/AA; 124br AA/P Wilson; 124/5b AA/AA; 125t AA/S McBride; 125bc AA/M Jourdan; 125br Illustrated London News.

Every effort has been made to trace the copyright holders, and we apologise in advance for any unintentional omissions or errors. We would be pleased to apply any corrections in a following edition of this publication.